D0620390

MY LIFE CLOSED TWICE

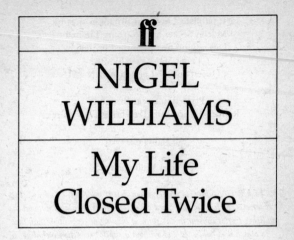

NIGEL WILLIAMS

My Life
Closed Twice

faber and faber
LONDON · BOSTON

First published in Great Britain in 1977 by
Martin Secker and Warburg Limited
This edition first published in 1986 by
Faber and Faber Limited
3 Queen Square London WC1N 3AU

Printed in Great Britain by
Redwood Burn Ltd, Trowbridge, Wiltshire

British Library Cataloguing in Publication Data

Williams, Nigel. *1948–*
My life closed twice.
I. Title
823'.914 [F]   PR6073.I4327

ISBN 0–571–14572–8

For
Suzan Harrison

My life closed twice before its close,
It yet remains to see,
If immortality unveil
A third event to me

So huge, so hopeless to conceive
As these that twice befell.
Parting is all we know of heaven
And all we need of hell.

Emily Dickinson

PART ONE

6.30 a.m. Monday

On most of them, you see, I want revenge. I want to make them suffer. Revenge first of all, on that guy at the publishers. I recall his letter as faithfully as I can. I can't bear to get it out from the pile.

> Dear Martin Steel,
>
> I'm afraid I'm returning *The Good The Bad and the Indifferent* to you. Some of us here liked it a lot, but none of us (alas!) enough to publish.
>
> Do let me see anything else of yours.
>
> Ronald Jones

Like your wife or your mother or your father. Just so long as it isn't a novel, short story, play or poem I'd love to see it. I mean— who does Ronald Jones think he is? What does he do on his free evenings? I can see him now—in a fetching leather bum-freezer—sitting with a few chosen friends in Charco's wine bar in Chelsea.

And who, while we're at it, are "some of us"? A sandpit full of trendies, up there in Bedford Square or wherever they hang out, lounging around like the last days of the Roman Empire and sneering at Manuscripts Received? Or is it just a stupid way of saying "Me"? Ronald Fucking Jones. Probably never even *tried* to write a novel. The ultimate one-upmanship.

Like the other week when I was with a Minor Poet, we met Davies, a zealous Talks Producer from Radio. It was about half past nine at night and the Minor Poet and I were having a steak

3

in the canteen, prior to recording some of his verse. There, at a table in the corner, was Davies, moustache drooping, stooped over a plate of soup.

"What goes on?" I asked.

"Oh," says Davies, "just doing some typing."

Suspicious. So I said, lightly and airily to the Minor Poet, as we made our way down to the studios,

"I bet he's writing a novel."

"Oh they're all writing novels at the BBC," says the Minor Poet, "only none of them are any good, are they?" And he looked at me keenly.

I knew then that he'd rumbled me. How in God's name does one conceal the fact that one writes novels? I really have tried to look as if I do something else with my leisure hours. I really have tried to *do* something else with my leisure hours actually but that's not the point. The fact or point is that I have written about fifteen novels in the last five years. About a million and a half words. And, all around my room, stuck to the walls, the ceiling, the floor even, are short, pithy letters on thick paper, all beginning "Dear Martin Steel" (why do they always use both names as if you were a kid at school?), and all of them saying, in one way or another— "Piss off with your bloody awful books." Here's another:

Dear Martin Steel,
            Yes I've read the two novels. I found *Down The Corridor* too long, and although I loved some of the dialogue and many of the set pieces from *The Jellabies Move To 22a Camden Hill Gardens*, I felt the joke didn't quite hold for two hundred pages!!!
                        Yours,
                        Elizabeth Jones

Elizabeth Jones. Probably a relation of Ronald's. Probably his sister. And what makes the thing so bad is that Elizabeth Jones is, or was, my agent. A woman greatly loved by other rattlesnakes in the Literary World because (quote) of her "in-built shit-detector". Sure she's got an in-built shit-detector—she detects shit and sells it to various publishers at enormous gain to herself.

4

Only the other rattlesnakes in the Literary World call this "being in touch with things".

Just a couple more letters before I get on with the business proper. One of the mealier variety from a creature who works (believe it or not) at the BBC. Last year, as a desperate resort, I took to writing for television. It seemed such an easy option. One simply writes "Interior. Day. Brighton." and there one is. I wrote a long (and quite funny) piece about a man who grows a pair of symbolic breasts and sent it to an acquaintance of mine from the Drama Department. Here is his reply:

> Dear Martin,
>
> Now you're really going to hate me for this! You see, I think *Serenade on a Rainy Day* is a good idea and a well written idea, but I think you haven't really come to terms with what television *wants* from a play (if you see what I mean). One has to do things that one feels it right to do now and I think that is the situation one is in here (really).
>
> If we want to be particular—I think that when David meets Julie on the station, from that moment on we really are unsure as to whether he is *only* doing this for Karen or whether his antics in the Department are a factor. And once that is exploded the whole David/Karen thing is no go.
>
> Agree?
>
> Paul
>
> P.S.   Let's meet and talk.

Let's not, Paul. Let's avoid each other for ten years, and, at the end of that period I will supervise a small but tasteful ceremony at which slices will be cut off your behind and served (with garlic bread) at a hootenanny for Script Editors. And, while we're at it Paul, when my sixteenth novel hits the bookstalls and you're catching up with my (unlisted) phone number—you will not get so much as an Italian meal out of me. When you ask for the Television Rights, I shall refer you to my new agent, a Greek half-wit from Camden Town, whose only other authors are world-famous playwrights and celebrities. I will make you crawl, Paul. Agree?

5

I'm coming on to the heart of the matter. Coming on to the point. One more letter from the pile. It is over by the cork-tipped noticeboard that Ellen put in when she thought I was going to be famous and I might need a cork-tipped noticeboard on which to pin the telegrams, contracts, postcards, etc. It is not headed. It is on blue paper. It is not typewritten. It is from a woman whom I will call, for the moment, by her real name. Julie. Hold on to that because I may call her something else in a moment. I may call her Bitchface or Cowfeatures or Fat—Anyway. This letter. It's dated and the date is quite a long time ago but you don't really need to know that either. It says:

> Dear Martin,
>   Please don't write to me any more. IT'S OVER. *Please*. I don't know about what's up with you. I don't really know anything about it at all. I'm sorry (I truly am) about what happened. But please. *Please*.
>   Love,
>   Julie
> P.S.   Would it have worked any way? I mean *ask* yourself.

You see the similarity of style? A rejection slip, whether sexual or literary, often uses the Arty Postscript. It is always written from a position of tremendous comfort and tremendous compassion. And it always makes the writer feel a hell of a lot better than the recipient. Thanks a lot Julie.

It's because of her that I've started writing this journal again, in the hopes that I'll get novel number sixteen out of it. And novel number sixteen will, *must* centre on me and Julie. I've put off writing about the only other woman in my life, apart from Ellen, for too long. It was realising how much I still hate her for what she did, that gave me the idea. I still want to have an effect on her, you see. I first started thinking of her yesterday afternoon when Ellen and I were in Brixton market. I saw a girl on the other side of the road who looked just like Julie, completely different class and age but the same bright eyes and the same hunched shoulders. And then, in spite of myself, the whole Julie thing came back to me, clear, sharp and painful. As we walked back up

Acre Lane I found I was rehearsing things I should have said to her, even staging rows in which I was disdainful, cruel and obviously right. Later on, in the pub, her face was still with me. I had to go up to my study and get something on paper straight away. But not a novel. Not yet. First, this journal, to conjure her up as she was, a place where I can relax and write what I like, the perfect setting for what the French call "the retort of the back stairs", which is the crushing reply you think up four hours after the host has insulted you, when you're leaving by the servants' staircase.

She was an incredibly good actor. I remember she played a boy once, in some play. Someone said to me in the interval "What do you think of Julie?" "Is she in it?" I replied. And then they told me she was playing the kid. I haven't seen her since . . . ah well, why go into all that. You couldn't say I *saw* her then. I'll use this journal, my daily ramblings, partly to work up a head of steam and partly to get material for a Julie character, raw stuff I can work up into a plot. If the novel should turn out to be a bestseller, I find myself imagining our meeting. Her attitude would have changed all right.

"Hi!"

"Hi!"

"Where's Ellen?"

"Oh . . . out you know . . ."

"Can I come in?"

"Sure." (I live now in a remote Irish village for tax purposes. Am loved and respected by the locals. "Dat's the wroither feller from England.")

"What a lovely house."

"Do you like it?"

"Mmm."

A pause. I show her the house and grounds. Then, at the door of the summerhouse, she says:

"I read your book."

"Did you?"

"Mmm."

"Did you like it?"

7

"Oh, Martin, you're so—"

"So what?"

"So hard. And yet not. In a way."

I move away from her and stare down at my private lough.
Lough Martin, or, as the locals call it, Lough Mairtinnnh.

"I know," I say.

"I just came to say ..."

"What did you come to say, Julie?"

"I came to say thank you, Martin."

Unable to control her emotion she hurries into the
summerhouse—forgetting to open the door first. Ha ha. Oh it's
nice thinking though. You see—some people are spoilt by
success, but I *know* it would only make me nicer, kinder, more fun
to be with. I suppose this book will be a way of buying back her
love, of making her notice me. Of somehow correcting all those
awful, awful mistakes of my adolescence.

So, here I am, not in a tax haven (yet), and miles away from
Julie, in my moderately well equipped home in Brixton, getting
up three hours before I have to go in to the office, forcing the
black coffee down me and hoping out of all this experience
something will come. Already I can see usable things. I'm sitting
at my desk, the rejection slips all round me—in the back garden
of the house opposite a mongrel dog is pacing like Hornblower on
his quarter deck, down across and back and down again. In a few
hours, maybe less, the West Indian next door will turn up Capital
Radio In Tune With London to superhuman levels of volume,
and Ellen will put her face round the door and look at me
sideways, elflike. Get on with it, Steel. Get on with it.

"I invented it."

"Terrific."

It turned out it was a mock-up of the tube destined to contain Chivalry, when the product finally went before the public. Morris had spent some two years producing this thing, for which he had been paid several thousand pounds. Once again I say it—what *happened* to us all?

Stavely eventually went abroad. All gone or dead or abroad. He is now teaching at a university in the Cameroons where the head of the department, an amiable savage, teaches an interesting course that includes The Novels of Shakespeare and The Plays of Joseph Conrad. I occasionally get long indecipherable airmail letters from the lad, who has taken two African women to wife and seems to spend most of his time zonked out on the local marijuana. When he went out there, of course, there was a lot of stuff about the third world and Fanon and how the multinationals must be ground into the dust, but, of late, his concerns have become more local—for a kickoff the fact that his second wife's family are *all* demanding jobs in the English faculty of the university, and, if employment is not forthcoming, he fears a primitive tribal vengeance will be wreaked. The fact that none of them can read doesn't seem to matter. When I think that for three years Stavely and Morris were the barrier between me and insanity, I feel guilty and contemplate ringing or writing or somehow repairing the horrid breach time and distance have made in our relationships—but it's too late. I prefer to think of them as they were, sitting in the corner of the King's Arms, eyes low over the Guinness. The wags.

Unfortunately I was not accompanied by any of them the first time I met Derek, in Julie's room in Bardwell Road. He was sitting in the corner by the bookcase, grinning like a yokel, in his lunch-hour. He wore a donkey jacket and jeans. When he was sitting down and I was standing up, I could just about reach his chin.

"This is Derek," said Julie furrily.

"Hullo Derek," I said.

"Hullo," said Derek. He had a deep depersonalised voice,

11

rather like that of an I-Speak-Your-Weight Machine. Julie watched him.

"Ciggies?" she said, in a coaxing, maternal voice. "How in God's name," she seemed to be thinking, "will this Ape manage to go out, buy a packet of cigarettes *and* come back all without being run over?"

"Ciggies?" she said again, suddenly switching from mother to child. Derek responded gladly to this. Like Frankenstein under remote control, he staggered to his feet and headed blindly for the door. Would he make it? By some miracle of coordination he managed to get one of his soup-plate-sized hands round the door handle and he tugged at it violently. Greatly to my surprise the door did not come away in his hands but slid back as if a normal person had opened it. Julie and I watched with bated breath as his colossal form teetered on the top stair. Did he know about stairs? we asked ourselves. He fell forward like a redwood tree and then stopped, leaning at an angle. Sharp intake of breath. Now you put your *left* foot forward, Derek, and. . . . As we watched, he did so, and, stiffly, like a much older man, headed off towards the hall and fresh dangers. Julie turned to me and smiled:

"Isn't he sweet?" she said.

"Terrific," I said, "but what happens when the battery runs out?"

"He's quite bright actually," said Julie, "and you mustn't be so nasty about people."

It's true that I never took Derek seriously. In the book I think he should start out like that, not exactly despised but ignored by my hero. Hovering at the edge of rooms, in the shadows, spilling things, tripping over furniture. . . . He wasn't (actually) unintelligent. I *think* they gave him a degree. Or maybe it was a Good Conduct Medal.

What happened when he came back with the fags though? And what did Julie and I say while he was out of the room? We went to the pub I remember that. But otherwise . . . You see just then I was up there, describing something, confident, seeing things, no worries, and now I've suddenly lost my nerve. What I need is not Derek but a fictional equivalent, someone who'll get up and walk about by himself. If I'm going to get that I need a name.

Arthur? No.

Peter? No.

Steve? No.

Roger?

Roger. Roger who? Roger Jones, Roger Smith, Roger ... Beamish. Roger Beamish.

POSSIBLE OPENING TO NOVEL NO.1

"Hullo!" said Roger Beamish.

"Hullo," I said.

Fine. So far so good. The characters fairly leap off the page at you don't they? "Mr Steel's characters have the quality of men and women trapped in wet cement." *The Guardian.*

And, while we're at it, I suppose we need a name for the me figure and for the girl who stands for Julie in all of this. If I used her real name she might sue. *Sue*—not a bad name....

POSSIBLE OPENING TO NOVEL NO.2

When Sue Faversham was twenty-one she fell in love with herself, quite suddenly, at a party in North Oxford. "The epigrams crackle like an old radio." *Books and Bookmen.*

And so on. Taking one's characters off the peg of life ought to be easy. But so often, the fictional version, with carefully altered name, hair, eyes, etc, ends up looking more like a tailor's dummy than the real thing. I remember when I was a kid, I bought, from The Largest Joke Shop in the World a mirror, that enabled you, or rather was intended to enable you, to draw like Picasso before he went funny. The machine, by means of a complex series of lenses, cast a shadow of the object intended to be drawn (a book, a chair, someone's face) and, said the advert, "ALL YOU HAVE TO DO IS DRAW A LINE ROUND IT!!! A CHILD CAN DO IT!!"

Well, a child could do it, although the simplest object ended up looking like a map of Gibraltar drawn under the influence of methylated spirit. The difficulty was, of course, that once you started to draw a line, you'd started to make something of your own. To pretend you were copying got you nowhere at all. So it is, I fear, with me and writing. I can see all the things, all the people, clearly in my head, but once I start to write them down or even when I become aware of the fact that I am writing them down instead of gossiping about them, I suddenly feel like a tightrope walker who's lost his nerve. I break off in the middle of a sentence and go scurrying back to Real Life with cries of "Let me down! Let me down!"

And, while I'm at this game of making the Julie thing into fiction, I suppose I need to find a name for the hero, the third point in the triangle. Unless I do it all in the first person. But even then I suppose characters would occasionally speak to me. An idea strikes me. Why don't I get someone else to write it? Nip into the Athenaeum one lunchtime and hand over the raw material to some alcoholic Man of Letters. Most of them have got nothing left to write about anyway—they need experience the way Dracula needed plasma, and I'm prepared to sign over the rights to my entire emotional history for the privilege of a mention in the Foreword. Any time. I only ever met one Great Writer. For years I'd been picking his paperbacks off the shelves of bookshops and asking myself "Why can't I write like this?" and then, quite by chance, I met him at a party given by, of all people, my aunt. He was sitting on the stairs by himself, and I talked to him for nearly an hour. I think he was the most boring guy I've ever met in my life—and, when I went back to his books, I found they'd been infected by his personality. All the epigrams conjured up for me was this fifty-year-old, oyster-eyed loser, droning on about How The Russians Were Taking Over. That's another danger of getting involved with the literary world. All of them seem to drift relentlessly towards the Right. The final move is when they write a long article in the *Daily Mail* attacking our great and glorious tax-laws—a sure sign that the auld alliance between Loot and Culture is flourishing. I think the writer I loathed most in my life

14

was a friend of my uncle's who'd written nearly fourteen books about the God-forsaken area of Northumberland in which he had had the misfortune to be brought up. He took me up to his study once and showed me all his volumes, spread out on the shelves:

"There!" he said, "my children!"

I looked around for small people. I saw none. I saw the books. I twigged. Before I had time to laugh, my uncle's friend had stuck his face into mine, had said:

"They'll be still here when bloody Wilson is rotting in his grave." He meant the Prime Minister, a man with whom he had somehow imagined I sympathised.

Ronald? Not really a Ronald. Or, to put it more accurately, I don't think that I *was* a Ronald because this story isn't about me now. It's about a place, a situation, I found myself in seven years ago. Dave? Was I a Dave? No. Not quite flashy enough. Charles? No. Not rich enough to be a Charles.

Stephen. Stephen Jarrett. Yes. That rather does things to me actually. I can see Stephen Jarrett quite clearly.

"Start on a shot of Oxford, seen from the train.... Gothic Cut Out at the end of a long stretch of level ground. Then, a high shot of a train, strung out, improbably blue and modern, like a toy in this last farmland before the town. Slowly we crane down until we are level with the windows, and track past families, jammed into facing seats, their picnic lunches spread out on the tables in front of them, past girls in headscarves, men with black briefcases, fat women in the prime of life, until we reach a boy in the corner seat of an empty compartment. He has a white, unhappy face, big bones and wide eyes. He's wearing a green corduroy jacket. He doesn't feel comfortable. He's staring out past the camera towards the town, a mixture of misery and hope. There is a large, white label hung round his neck which says 'STEPHEN JARRETT: IST-YEAR UNDERGRADUATE: VIRGIN'."

That was me folks! And I can hear the readers mutter: "Oh yeah!" as they turn the page and wonder what's on the telly. "What else?" Well, I'm afraid that they'll just have to put up with the fact that some of the book, or rather most of it, will take place in Oxford, and that some of the characters will be virgins.

Due to the fact that I was at Oxford and a virgin for an impossibly long time. The trouble is, of course, that people nowadays don't want books about Oxford. They want books about Rugby League players with crushes on each other. Which is absurd since the book-buying public (all three of them) went to Oxford or Cambridge, and do not *know* the rules of Rugby League.

It's the old problem of my life being something of a literary cliché. I didn't know this, of course, while I was living it. But you've got to remember that when I was swotting for my O-levels and trying to pick up girls at Golders Green Bus Station, I didn't know I was going to be a novelist. If I had, I would have got on with the business of having a mental breakdown, seeing the world or being buggered by men in Hyde Park. All of the things that make for interesting reading. I mean, even all that's a cliché these days so where that leaves a lad who went to Public School, University and then the B.B. fucking C. I don't know. Here I suppose.

Like everyone else, I drifted into my job. I'm the lowest of the low in television circles, my technical description "researcher". I work on a programme that allegedly deals with politics but is in fact a buffet cum publicity service for Ministers of the Crown. I had this idea at the back of my mind that Television Centre was packed with young, nubile girls of the kind you see in *Top Of The Pops*, just waiting for young men to ease into their lives. Well—it's full of girls all right, but not the kind you see on *Top Of The Pops*. Those they fabricate at a warehouse in Deptford, rubberised and ready lubricated, they are brought down to the studios in huge black vans under cover of night, and shipped back stealthily after the recording. The girls you get at Television Centre are twenty-eight-year-old ladies who have hitchhiked to Australia, had two affairs and are now keen to Settle Down. And the kind of person they want to settle down with is me. If it hadn't been for Ellen I'd be lumbered with some cleverly disguised harpy out in Twickenham, discussing my career every night.

No, television, like so many supposedly glamorous professions, is full of people who ought to be selling cars for a living. These same people, by dint of persistent bootlicking and the signing

16

over of their brains to the company, have achieved what is some-times termed control of the Media. Actually, if you could see the people who control the Media, all conspiracy theories, whether of the Left or of the Right, would pale into insignificance. Television Man isn't a cunning and unscrupulous fiend manipulating the medium for his own ends—he is usually a half-wit, a sort of technological valet, a flunkey to a machine he does not understand. The funniest thing in the world is to be in the gallery of a television studio, when something goes wrong.

Picture it. A large, darkish room with a semi-circular desk, opposite which are a row of monitors, very much in the style of the Starship Enterprise, and, seated in swivel chairs, facing these screens—The Team. The director, usually a svelte, Arts-based youth, observing that all the screens have gone blank or that smoke is coming out of a camera, turns to another, older man, seated at the opposite end of the desk, and says: "Problem." The older man is the Technician. He then picks up a telephone and dials another (possibly even older) man and says: "We have a problem." There is then silence for some minutes. At the end of this, a pallid creature comes from one of the many mysterious doors that lead off from the gallery of the studio. No one seems to recognise him. Is he the man phoned by the Technician? This is never explained. He says: "We tried kicking it." The Technician nods remorsefully. Then the pallid man disappears. The director yawns.

The awful truth dawns on the casual observer. *No one in the place knows anything about how any of the equipment works*. They are in the position of Australian aborigines flying a Jumbo Jet. The real heroes of the medium are the Germans who designed the whole thing in the first place—but they are all far away, getting on with the schedule for World War Three.

I digress. I mustn't talk about my job. My job is irrelevant. As from tomorrow, I've taken two weeks' holiday to try and get this novel finished. So why let that alien world intrude. Why think about my Professional Life, or lack of it. I'm talking about my emotional life, my past, my rich store of experience that will strike a chord in so many other twenty-seven-year-old hearts.

17

What makes my life so unique is that I have *not* been a short-order cook, lumberjack, pirate or strolling musician.

And there must be no defeatist talk. There is a book there, I know there is. It happened to me, and something like it happens to other people. All I have to do is to go back, remember it, get it right, and then conjure a story out of it. What she did to me and what I did to her. The thought occurs to me that there were faults on both sides. Come on then—I summon up the past.

3

Will I get fan letters when the book is published? Will I? I ask myself this question as I stare out through the net curtains.

Dear Martin Steel,
      I red yore book about you and the girl and me and my sister age 21 would like to kum and fuck the shit out of you. I am 18, blonde and with big breasts. I enclose "photo" to prove it.

                Laura Jones

That's the kind of fan letter I'd like. I did once get one but it wasn't like that. It went: P.S. When is your play on?

And that came at the end of a ten-page description of the writer's holiday in France.

The writer was a girl called Elinor. Elinor and I met at a wine and cheese party given by the Totteridge Young Conservatives. There were hardly any Young Conservatives there in fact—it was mainly North London desperadoes, looking for a bit of spare. Elinor was about the closest thing to a Young Conservative in the room—sartorially and ideologically. She was a broad-shouldered wench, much given to funny voices, and still in love with her father. She and I went to the pictures together every Saturday night for nearly a year, and occasionally kissed at parties. I think I was in the sixth form at school. At the end of this time, a friend of mine came up to me at one of these parties and said:

"Mart, I've got some bad news."

"Oh God," I said. I thought someone had died.

"It's Elinor," said the friend, "she doesn't want to go out with you any more—"

I gaped.

"She's really scared of hurting you," said the friend.

At which, I'm afraid I felt a desire to burst out laughing. All I could think about was the immense saving in cinema tickets. The only question in my mind was—what had made her terminate the affair? Should I have proposed marriage? The question was answered later in the party when I saw her hanging on the neck of a youth almost as ugly as me. Maybe he's still going to the cinema with her. Who knows? The last I heard was the letter mentioned above, referring to a work of mine called *The Unlearning Of Love* staged for one night by an amateur dramatic company in the winter of 1968.

I am seriously thinking of putting Elinor in the book, thinly disguised as a Wimpy Bar Attendant in the Cowley Road. She may well be run over by an articulated lorry while in her attractive Wimpy Bar Attendant costume. I don't want to go into the whole fan-letter thing, but the thought occurred to me during one of those frequent breaks in transmission from which my brain seems to suffer. I was staring out at the black lady opposite, who was hauling in the family smalls on a rather ingenious pulley-system clothesline and wondering whether I should put *her* in the novel. That led me on to wondering whether I should work a bit of Social Relevance into the book, which brought me back to the What Will They Make Of It and Will They Publish It department. From there to fan letters and eighteen-year-old girls. I've never had an eighteen-year-old girl. When I was eighteen they were all screwing guys of twenty-six and now I'm twenty-six they're all screwing guys of eighteen. Bitches.

That's probably why at the time at which I went to Oxford I was walking around with an almost permanent hard-on, which I could only get rid of after prolonged sessions of self-abuse. From time to time I drew blood. I think I'd got to the awkward stage where nothing could satisfy me except intercourse with a real live woman. When I first met Julie, I remember thinking "Well, she's not exactly *pretty*, but she's very sexy and well within my price range." She had straight, rather greasy hair, big eyes and a puckered-up, old maid's mouth. But, with all this there was something curiously glamorous about her, an assurance I'd never seen in any of the other girls I knew. Which is why, I suppose, I walked across the floor to talk to her.

We were both extras in this amazingly trendy outdoor production of *King Lear*, being rehearsed in a gymnasium in the Cowley Road.

"Hullo!"

"Hi!"

We sat against the wall, clutching our knees.

"What are you?" said Julie.

"Oh," I said, "I'm a spear carrier really."

"Me too," said Julie, "except ladies don't carry spears really do they?"

"Jug carrier then," I said.

She grinned.

"*Lovely*."

I watched her carefully. Little by little, the tension relaxed, and we both felt able to watch the rehearsal. Then, into a rapt, mutual silence, Julie said:

"I should like to have a long part with a *lot* of lines."

"Mmm."

"Don't you think that would be nice?"

"I do."

I clammed up on her then. It's true that I don't like women to take too much of the initiative. I have a secret fear that the female sex has taken out a contract on my balls. But we walked back from the rehearsal together, and we saw a lot of each other in the weeks leading up to the performance.

The director, Jan Darrow, wanted to take the show to the Mynack Theatre in Cornwall, which, in case you didn't know, is a kind of amphitheatre at the top of a three-hundred-foot cliff. He had conceived the amusing notion of doing it in the open air in late November, to really get the feeling of Man against the Elements. The idea was that people would come well wrapped up and carrying Thermos flasks. Darrow, a small, fat postgraduate studying Chinese, said they would discover a new dimension in the play. Unfortunately, on the opening night, Kent fell through a fissure in the rocks and plunged three hundred feet to his death. Unjokey. While Air Sea Rescue combed the bay below we blundered on, in the finest traditions of the Oxford Experimental Theatre Company. The reviews were devastating. "King Lear," said one critic, "looked as if he had piles." This was unsurprising as the actor playing Lear did actually have piles. He spent too much of the play seated on a stone throne wearing only a luminous jock strap. Julie and I were very much background figures, and were thus able to spend long hours in a caravan getting to know each other.

As I'd guessed at the rehearsal, Julie was a girl with an Interesting Past. She was very coy about it in those early stages. All she'd say was that at some point she'd spent six months in Vienna having an unhappy love affair. I was enormously impressed by this. She was amusing, vaguely mysterious and out of reach, quite unlike the girls I'd met outside the Ionic in Golders Green. We travelled home in the train together, by which time my cock had developed rigor mortis. After a tentative farewell kiss on the platform it was back to Mummy and Daddy for me. Christmas vacation. And, I discovered afterwards, it was in the Christmas vacation that she met Derek. So, for the three millionth time, I can blame my parents.

QUIZ ... THIS QUIZ SHOULD BE ATTEMPTED ONLY BY THE ASTUTE READER. ALTHOUGH WHY ARE YOU READING ALL THIS? IT'S PRIVATE!!!!

Are my Mummy and Daddy:

  a) Northern Working Class who do not understand their clever son?
  b) Rich Aristocratic Shits with an interesting lifestyle?
  c) Middle Class Casualties just like their clever son?

ALL YOU HAVE TO DO!!!

Is guess which of the three they are from the following piece of badly remembered dialogue and you win a free literary lunch at Foyles together with a coffee table edition of

The Soft Machine by William Burroughs. *Plus* a weekend in Paris at the Hotel of your choice with Philip Toynbee OR Raymond Williams. HURRY HURRY WHILE CRITICS LAST!!!!

I opened the door.

"Oh," said my mother, coming from the stairs, "Oh." There was something wild and Brontë-like about her eyes.

"Daddy's gone up to Lipton's," she said, in the tone of a newsreader announcing some colossal natural disaster. Then—in the same Gothic-horror style: "The boiler's gone wonky."

"Oh," I said.

"Yes," said Ma, "yes. It's the anthracite. The anthracite's all funny."

I remember standing there feeling that old helpless family feeling, the feeling of being stuck in a small canoe, far out in the Pacific Ocean with a group of monolingual Latvians, the feeling that no conversation about *anything* serious would ever be possible.

WELL? HOW DID YOU DO? EASY WASN'T IT?

My parents aren't, actually, an irrelevant joke, but I find it difficult to think of them otherwise. And impossible, at the moment, to write about them otherwise. I think if I had been able to talk to them about Julie, the way some kids seem to talk to their parents, I wouldn't have fucked the whole thing up in quite the way I did. With my friends, you see, the rules were to keep very cool about these matters—wags did not admit to tender feelings. All that Christmas vacation I sat around, not daring to ring her, not knowing how to behave with a girl who was (possibly) as brainy as me. While my family? They continued to discuss the boiler at great length.

The boiler was, in fact, the centre of the Steel family life. It was at the time a Zebedee Solid Fuel Z.496 Boiler with Hopper Gravity Feed. When it was installed, the man said that it had to be "topped-up" at night, and, occasionally, in the mornings. "A simple job," he said as he left, to be seen no more. What he meant was that at all hours of the day and night, a member of the family had to be by its side pouring anthracite down its throat and crooning at it gently in case the said anthracite got stuck in its tum-tum. It was a huge, blue and red structure, squatting in the middle of what Ma still calls "the laundry". I think it's worth a few pages in the novel. Rather lyrical in tone I fancy.

And, while I'm on that first Christmas vacation, I'd better get the boot into the old man good and proper. I loathe those sentimental, cloying pieces, with titles like *Father and Son* or *My Dad*, in which the author, whether he be Edmund Gosse or John Mortimer, sifts through the ten or twelve years of sheer hell that growing up under another male must always be, for some spark of sentiment. It usually turns out that they hated him for twelve years, and then, for five minutes at the top of the Brenner Pass or somewhere, they saw a dewdrop on the end of his moustache, realised He was Mortal, and forgave all. What's so sickening about all that, usually, is that it's an acknowledgment by the deadbeat that he proposes to make exactly the same mistakes as Dad.

No, my old man feels about me the way Goebbels felt about the Jews, and I feel about him the way the Jews felt about Goebbels. And he won't be spared. Everything will be there—the Accountancy, the driving in the middle of the road, the unhealthy obsession with Golf, and the Puritanism. I toy with the idea of making him a Seventh Day Adventist who has been thrown out of the sect for being too much of a hardliner. And, in the middle of all these monsters—me. I can't describe the complete confusion I felt when I returned to Oxford late that January. I was desperate to screw Julie, but (complicated this) I wanted to see her again because I liked talking to her. I was frightened of her, a little, I despised her, a little—there was no one I could talk to without pretending to be tougher than I was.

In the train going up I sat next to a man who was writing mathematical symbols on the back of an envelope; walking from the station it was misty, and, outside the Nag's Head an Irishman

24

was leaning unsteadily against the wall. When I got back to the college, Stavely and Morris were waiting for me in my room. They had taken a corduroy jacket that I'd left over the vac, stuffed it full of paper and laid it out on the bed, arms outstretched. On the pillow, above the jacket, they had placed a cabbage, and, on top of the cabbage, a deerstalker hat. Beneath the jacket, splayed at an angle, a pair of Stavely's trousers, also loosely stuffed, and, beneath the trousers—a pair of socks. Into the left-hand side of the jacket they had fixed an arrow, just above where the heart would have been. They had opened a bottle of port I had hidden under one of the radiators when drunk.

"It's because you're in love," said Morris.

"Oh," I said.

Stavely opened his eyes very wide.

"It took us four hours to do!" he said.

"Thanks," I said, "thanks a lot."

Later that night I went up to Bardwell Road and stood opposite the house where she lived. Nobody came in—nobody went out. When I got back, feeling cold and light-headed, Stavely and Morris had gone out to the pub. The dummy was untouched, except that, before leaving, they had sellotaped a peeled banana onto the fly-buttons—it was leaning out crazily, just erect. I ate it all, right down to the sellotape, and sat in the room alone, not bothering to turn on the light. I think at some stage I wrote a poem—not a very good one.

Oh Julie, Julie, I didn't stand a chance against you did I?

4

Talking of standing a chance against people, Ellen just put her face round the door. First a nose, then two huge eyes, then the edge of a foot. She looked at me, doing her impression of Bambi meeting the white hunter.

"Hullo!" I said.

"Hullo!" she whispered, switching to the Servant Girl in the Presence of the Great Writer. Which, of course, manoeuvred me into the position of having to acknowledge the fact that I'm not a Great Writer, any more than she's Bambi or a Servant Girl.

Once she'd got our respective rôles thoroughly in doubt, she felt it safe to enter the room. She was wearing the red T-shirt that just covers her crotch. I turned from the desk and watched her. She folded her lips over her teeth, imploded her mouth and lengthened her face by about six inches. This, combined with the fact that she widened her eyes into a goldfish-like stare, made her look like something out of a Charles Addams cartoon. Then she stuck her bum in the air and did an impression of someone walking the wrong way along a conveyor belt. Then she went out. Point taken. I read you Red T-shirt. As I write I hear a manic cackle from next door. The next stage is Mint Tea.

As I was saying, dear, before you interrupted me, I went back to Oxford somewhat confused. And, the first day back, went up to see Julie. That was when I met Derek for the first time. But the joke was that I wasn't at all worried about him. I was mainly worried about that mysterious past of hers. She had been, and, in a way, still was, hung up on a guy called Harris, a poet, athlete and wit, who'd treated her, as far as I could make out, very much as an old boot or shoe. I can remember her talking about Harris, in pubs, on the bus, in cinema queues; he was the guy, it turned out, who'd given her the baby that she'd dumped in Florence. And, when she talked about him, I got visions of a kind of Adonis, cruel, witty and perfect. Which, of course, only made Julie more attractive and more unobtainable. I actually met Harris some four years after the Julie thing was over, in a lunchtime theatre in Ealing. Far from being a superman, Harris turned out to be a broken-backed midget who Wanted to Write. But that was always Julie's way. People who had had a poem published in their old school magazine were described as "writers", French teachers at obscure preparatory schools as "brilliant linguists", and unemployed drug addicts as "film directors". She didn't need rose-tinted glasses, she had a rose-tinted brain.

But, all that second term, I swallowed it. All of it. And I listened to hours and hours of chat about Harris. Or, rather, Derek and I did. The three of us used to go to a pub in St Aldate's called the Bulldog, and she'd hold forth on the subject of Harris. Where Was He Now? Why Did He Treat Her So Mean? And so on. . . . If Derek had had more of a sense of humour maybe I would have looked across at him just once and smiled and we would both have realised the absurdity of the situation. But he hadn't and I didn't. She had both of us absolutely where she wanted us.

On one occasion, I remember, I took her to a Ball in the Union Building, for which I borrowed a dinner jacket from one Hundke, a wizened Jewish Social Democrat with whom I shared a room. She spent the whole evening talking about Harris—his eyes, his skin, his way with the cutting epigram. After the ball was over we repaired to my room, where I attempted to remove her top. This proved hopeless. She lay across my lap, staring up at the ceiling, and recited the following poem, composed by her in honour of Harris:

> "Bend over, he said,
> Your breasts are like melons.
> And I?
> I believed his lies,
> And wasted the eternal night."

And lies they certainly were, unless Harris had never ever come across a decent-sized melon. In the end I did manage to get one of them out, and after pummelling it for some moments, was rewarded by a description of her abortion. Evenings with Julie à deux usually followed that pattern. I got to look forward to having Derek around. At least, then, we didn't get the poems. And the arguments. To cope with the emotional front I'd started to drink fairly heavily, spending large amounts of time in the college bar, a kind of academic Skid Row, where huge Celts, puzzled by their subjects, drank themselves into a stupor every night. Sometimes Derek would join me on these expeditions.

A prickteaser. Unpleasant phrase. But that's what Julie was. Because there was always just enough to keep you around. She gave a little more each time. I remember that we were in Darrow's last play for the E.T.C. It was a production of *Hamlet* in which, in order to "de-mythologise" the text, Darrow had cut Hamlet out of the play. He had also developed slightly off-centre notions of the rôle of the audience—instead of allowing them to sit in chairs and watch, he herded them into a kind of circle and we prowled around the edges, shouting at them. It was at the first night party for this affair (which, incidentally, was a great success) that Julie promised, or *sort* of promised, to sleep with—

"Heh. Heh. Heh."

Damn. Ellen is now cackling on the landing. I am faced with three possibilities. I go out and make advances to her. I go out and reason with her. Or I stay here and continue to work on the novel.

Possibility number one ... well, there's no guarantee she'll come across. The cackling could be a prelude to what I have christened the Witch of Endor routine. This involves a hunching of the shoulders, a pulling of the red T-shirt very, very low, almost to knee level, and a scuttling away, crabwise, down the stairs. Very larky. Possibility number two (reasoning with her):

Me: Darling—

Ellen (straightening up from hunchback position and looking super-normal):

Yes darling?

Me: It's just that I'm trying to work...
Ellen: Yes darling.
Me: O.K?
Ellen: Fine. Fine.
Me: Great, love.

(I turn. Immediately my back is turned she reverts to the Quasimodo position.)

Ellen: Heh heh heh!!!

Hopeless. Which leaves me with option three. The which I am following. Sitting here and ... she has given up. I hear her go down the stairs and start to run a bath. From now on it will be difficult to get peace. If Ellen is running the bath, then it must be seven or half past which leaves very little time until the radio. "And the next record is for Ellen and Martin Steel of Brixton. Ellen would like to exchange her husband for an avocado pear. If anyone can help could they ring her on 733-1601 ..." And, after the radio—Oswald. I must resist the temptation to put Oswald in the novel. Oswald is after all a *friend* as well as a lodger, and, although it's hard to resist the temptation to describe him (since he would be *terrific* in a novel), I am resisting it. On with the book.

Coming back to question of style. I suppose I can only get a style once I've made up my mind about the significance of the raw material. I'm not really sure whether it's funny or stupid or just plain sad. Just at the moment I feel sorry for myself or, if you like, sorry for Stephen Jarrett, sitting on a bed with a cheap print cover, her lying across him reading awful poems. What a waste. What a waste.

The answer has to be—I want to hurt her. I do want to hurt her. To draw blood, perhaps to prove to myself that there is still blood in both her and me. If we met at a party now we could probably screw, no questions asked. We could do what we couldn't do then—satisfy each other, because our appetites have shrivelled. And I want to hurt her and myself back into feeling. I want to hate her enough for that. I want to have the courage of my convictions. I don't want to feel marooned in a fog of charity. Because my former self wants to hurt her, Stephen wants to hurt her, Stephen, with her on his knee under the bare light bulb

29

wants to rip off her dress, scratch her face until she's screaming with pain, and shout "FOR GOD'S SAKE BELT UP ABOUT FUCKING HARRIS!!"

But I didn't begin like that. I sat there, and, after a while, I put her breast back into its drab, nylon cup and she did her hair in the mirror and we walked up the Banbury Road to the Parks, turned right into Bardwell Road, and, in the damp, nostalgic Oxford evening, went up to her room, talked about books we'd read, drank coffee (of course) and maybe listened to records. Lovin' Spoonful, early Beatles, Beach Boys—all with something helpful to say to a teenager in my situation, badly dressed, too clever by half and hopelessly, hopelessly in love with a girl called Julie.

I've doubled back on myself. I'd got to the bit where she had sort of promised to sleep with me. The problem was—I was never quite sure whether she was going to sleep with me or Derek or both of us at the same time. I think (and this was part of her having a rose-tinted brain) she saw the three of us as a Jules et Jim style ménage. But, not being a thirty-year-old Frenchwoman, she was unable to stop herself bitching about Derek with me, and, presumably, about me with Derek. And although Derek and I liked each other well enough, we were always made to feel a little too much rivals. I suppose adolescents can be very cruel. She knew very well what would happen if she gave us too much rope.

I can remember another Ball, not the Union affair, where she made another of those guarded clever promises that kept me hanging on. We were in a "sitting-out" room—a freezing, underfurnished hovel attached to some college buildings. Some ball organiser had hung scraps of coloured paper across the ceiling—there was a table littered with cutlery, and, at the edge of the table, as a gesture towards good cheer, someone had left three prawn cocktails. Julie rubbed my knee in a sisterly fashion:

"You know what, Martin?"

"What?"

"You're awfully nice really."

"Oh. Thanks."

30

She looked at me sideways.

"If only you wouldn't go on so."

"Go on about what?"

"You know what."

"Oh. That."

"Yes. That."

I shifted uncomfortably.

"Well..."

"Listen," she said, "all things come to those who wait."

"Ah."

Another couple came in, the youth sunk in gloom at having paid three quid for a free glass of wine and a prawn cocktail, the girl sunk in gloom at being with such a mean guy. The girl picked up a prawn cocktail and started to munch it. The lettuce made a curiously harsh sound in the empty room. After she'd munched for about a minute, the youth drifted off, mumbling "...er... bog...think I'll..." I realised he was drunk. The girl put down her glass and followed him. Julie and I were alone. I turned to her and kissed her as hard as I could, trying to hurt her. I was sure that it needed only a little more pushing and I'd be there— Derek, Harris, all these absurd competitors would be out of the way. She'd said it, hadn't she? "Everything comes to those who wait."

The thing rather exploded in our faces at the beginning of the summer term. And that's one scene I can't help remembering for the novel. Even if, at times, I wish I could forget...

As I recall, I was carrying the hamper. We were on the east side of the Cherwell, about a hundred yards up from the boathouse. Julie began by lying full length, looking up at the sky in her "I'm a Victorian Child" manner. Annoyingly enough, I found it rather attractive. Derek had wandered off to the other end of the field. I looked at the river and I looked at her. She propped herself up on one arm.

"Isn't it *lovely*, here?"

"Mmm."

She eyed me. That's the only way I can describe it. So I eyed her back. We could carry on this sort of thing for any length of

31

time. Once again I rehearsed possible seduction intros. Gaze at her for two or three minutes more, then walk casually across to her, place the hand on the breast and—

"Oh look—Derek's found something!"

"Oh. Great!"

Derek had indeed found something. He could be seen stooping against the skyline, some fifty yards away. Not for the first time that day I prayed that he might wander a little further. Possibly towards the by-pass. Even if he were not involved in a road accident, there was always the chance that he might bang his head on a low bridge. Julie brought her knees up under her chin and hugged them in girlish excitement.

"He has," she said, "he *has*. He's picking something up."

A mine perhaps, I thought. An unexploded mine. I got the bottle of wine out of the hamper and began to screw the corkscrew down. Deep into Derek's bollocks, I twisted—and *again*, and *again* and *again* and how does that feel, Derek? And how does *that* feel?

"You are sweet," said Julie.

That word again. She was always telling me I was sweet. Not good. I wrenched my mouth sideways in an effort to unsweeten it, but she's stopped watching me. She was lying on her stomach, artily chewing a piece of grass and looking over towards Derek, who'd started on the long trek home. He rolled slightly as he walked, like a sailor coming out of the harbour into the main street.

"Well, Julie," I said, spreading a white cloth out next to the hamper, and sorting through greasy slices of mortadella as if they were playing cards, "today's going to be a great day."

She appeared to change her mind about something because she did a sudden switch from her Victorian Child manner. She got to her feet, crossed towards me and put her hand on my knee, squatting unathletically in front of me.

"Martin," she said, "you and Derek—"

"Yes?" I said.

All she had to do was *slide* the hand down the leg, unzip the flies, and tweak out the penis, already pounding like a

32

sledgehammer at the underpant cavity wall. And then all I had to do was—

"Oh. It doesn't matter," she concluded, sighing into my eyes, "it doesn't matter."

At this moment, with both of us gazing into each other's eyes, the sky around us began to darken and the earth to shake perceptibly. At first I thought this might have something to do with our physical proximity. Then I suspected it might be a cement mixer. It was, in fact, Derek, standing above us and smiling down in his best lovable Bonehead manner. As we looked up at him the smile turned into a look of vague distress and compassion.

"What was it?" said Julie.

"What was what?" replied Derek.

"What you found," she said.

"Dead rabbit."

"Oh *no*."

This was more than I could take, and, disengaging myself from Julie, I got up and started to sort through the hamper. Julie on the subject of nature was bad enough, but on the subject of our Dumb Chums, she was insufferable. To me animals should be either pulling things, donating their skins or fleeces to the cause of human warmth or else lying in slices upon plates, surrounded by the appropriate vegetables. I felt that Julie, on the other hand, would like to see them all in blue linen jackets, carrying spades and singing tiny, tiny songs. At any moment, I thought, one or other of them will suggest burying the thing.

"We can't let it lie there," said Julie.

"Why on earth not?" I asked.

"Because not . . . I don't know why not."

"Rabbits are expendable."

"And you're a pig."

"Fine."

I stood slightly apart from them, a large piece of French bread in my hand. I felt suddenly exposed.

"I thought I was supposed to be sweet."

Derek seemed embarrassed by all this. Often, now I think of it, in those early days, Derek adopted the rôle of peacemaker between me and Julie. He looked at Julie with tolerant amusement.

"O.K., Julie, if you insist."

As he said this, he winked at me, as if to say "*Women.*" Had I been a woman, I would have found the whole thing impossibly heavy-handed, but Julie seemed to enjoy being treated like a child, although I don't think I've ever met anyone as lethally mature as she was.

"I'll get on with this," I said.

And so, the rodent's funeral cortège moved off across the field. I watched them pick the thing up and then wander rather hopelessly towards the wood at the edge of the field, Derek holding it at arm's length. They looked like something out of *The Wizard of Oz*—Derek's huge, jacketed form (he always wore formal clothes even in the hottest weather) and Julie, tiny and active, skipping ahead of him. If she had held his hand you would have taken them for father and daughter. When I got bored with watching them, I sat down and addressed myself to the wine. Curiously enough, I was easier in my mind now she wasn't actually with me. The Julie problem was essentially a biological one. In a way it was nice not to have her there, not to feel the constant need to be amusing, to be on one's guard, to be *just* nice enough to Derek. I stretched out on the grass and wondered whether dead rabbits carried any dangerous diseases.

How long does it take to bury a rabbit? Assuming, that is, you have no spade or other implement? I had no idea. But it doesn't take fifteen minutes. And, after fifteen minutes, I became, mildly, alarmed. It was just possible that Derek was arguing his case, and putting a seduction campaign into operation, although the idea of Derek seducing anybody was frankly laughable. The other alternative was that something really had happened to them both. I got up. They were nowhere in sight. Leaving the picnic behind me, I set off across the field, my jersey across my shoulder. There was no rabbit, no Derek, and no Julie at the end of the field. And, by now beginning to be genuinely worried, I pushed my way into the wood, calling her name at first and then not, because I felt scared, alone and unanswered.

I practically stepped on them, but they didn't see me. First of all I saw Derek's huge, white rump pumping into her and then Julie's face over his left shoulder, eyes rolled up into her head, gasping for breath and her fingers drilled into his back, as if she were dying. They had been in too much of a hurry to take off more than was absolutely essential—the only thing I saw was her tights around a gorse bush, two yards to the left, and these two bodies stuck together obscenely, like—

CAPITAL RADIO ONE NINE FOUR YOU GET ALL THE HITS AND MORE!!! HULLO IT'S IAN DAVIDSON HERE BRINGING YOU A SPECIAL GUEST TO THE MORNING SHOW! HARRY SALTZMANN HAS ONLY BEEN IN THE COUNTRY FOR THREE HOURS AND HERE HE IS FOR YOU AND ONLY YOU—

Psschreaiewou!! Bath number two has started. Thump thump thump. Oswald going down to see if the papers have arrived.

BUT I ONLY HAVE EYEEEZ FOR YEEOUW! ART GARFUNKEL SAYS HE ONLY HAS EYES FOR YOU AND CERTAINLY I KNOW HOW HE FEELS ON THIS PARTICULAR MORNING BECAUSE WITH ME IN THE STUDIO IS A MAN WHO KNOWS MORE ABOUT THE OBJECT OF YOUR DREAMS THAN ALMOST ANYONE ELSE IN THE—

Bang! Crash! Door creak ... and thwaackk as the papers hit the mat. Ellen crashes out of the bathroom. Is coming up the stairs. Oswald crashes out of his bathroom. Bath not ready yet. One step two step three step four. They meet on the landing outside my room. No footsteps. I stare at the manuscript of this journal. They are talking. Soft whispers. Goblin confidences being exchanged? Well?

Once again I turn from my desk as, for the second time this morning, the door opens very, very slowly, to a distance of about a foot. At a height of three feet up off the floor, Ellen's head appears—a disembodied grin, like the Cheshire Cat's. I nod and smile. Three feet higher up again, in similar fashion, as if it had been poked through the aperture on a stick, appears Oswald's head, resembling that of a troll who has recently discovered treasure. I watch both heads, gravely.

"Hullo," says Ellen's head.

35

"Hullo," I say.

"Hullo," says Oswald's head.

"Hullo," I say.

"Time to get up!" say both heads.

It is. Time to leave my old self. Time to leave Stephen Jarrett
or whatever I'm going to call him. Time to get to grips with my
life again. I've got so much better at that since I was at Oxford,
since I was the boy on the page. Haven't I? Haven't I?

5

Hmm. A few days have gone by since I wrote anything in this journal. But exciting days. Probably because (miraculously) the novel started to take off. Maybe it was taking a holiday. Maybe it was remembering me stumbling over Julie having a fuck with a giant that got me going. I've written about twenty thousand words, and Julie and Derek are in there, at times rather too thinly disguised for comfort. But that can be changed. It *is* good I think. And it is a bit better than my other stuff. You see—my big problem has always been how to universalise things. How to get away from what has always seemed to me to be the curse of English fiction—dreary, line by line naturalism. Who did what to whom in N.W.1. Or—in this case—Oxford (even more of an obvious venue for thwarted love). What our fiction seems to me to lack is style, an authentic voice that *creates* incident. Too much of it is *only* incident, stitched together by smart remarks. What I am going to do in this novel (and this journal helps incredibly here) is to hold the facts in my head but never allow them to drown my voice. I've got a narrator figure, an elderly statesman guy, who's seen the world and speaks with authority. He's telling the story of a cousin of his called Sue Faversham, a girl he knew vaguely at Oxford years ago. Her story, and that of two youths who were in love with her (Stephen Jarrett and Roger Beamish). The novel is cast, after the manner of *Heart of Darkness*, in the form of an after-dinner story, and, at the moment there's a vague suggestion that my narrator is in a club or some other relic of the English Establishment. It's cast more in the form of a speech for the prosecution than a story, and I've made the man's style mirror the characters he's describing—soft and slushy for Julie, hard for Stephen, and jerky and deliberately confused for Derek. James Joyce Rules O.K. *I think* I may sketch in the narrator figure more closely. Later on.

It's not surprising, really, that the Derek and Julie Fuck Eavesdrop axis should have been so significant. After all, it was about the closest I had come to the sexual act in all my nineteen years of life. I might well never have recovered, condemned to a lifetime's voyeurism, haunting low bars, unable to hold down a job, always in front of me the nightmare memory of Derek's bum moving with the speed and precision of a steam hammer.

I can't concentrate on the manuscript today. Actually. Not because it reminds me of the Painful Past. Not because I think the fucking scene doesn't work—in fact I was that naïve, in the way only clever adolescents can be. I seemed to have no conception of where I ended and other people began. *But*—largely because I seem to have lost it. The manuscript, that is. Or rather—it has been stolen. I am at the moment the victim of a systematic campaign of disruption and dislocation led by Ellen and aided and abetted (I am almost sure) by Oswald. Their aim is, I would guess, to stop me finishing the book. This may sound absurd, and even slightly paranoid, but I do know that Ellen has always been jealous of my talent. Indeed she often says, when we're discussing it, "What talent?" I usually manage to laugh and shrug it off, but, of late, with my score of rejection slips reading 729, this has become more difficult. I suppose she read that letter from that Scottish theatre rejecting a play I sent them four years ago. I've puzzled over the letter for some time and am unable to decide whether it is or isn't a brilliantly sadistic, deadpan, black joke. It goes:

Dear Martin Steel,
       Sorry to have taken so long about reading your play but we are rather behindhand. I found it quite interesting. Have you any new stuff that we could see?
       Regards,
        Peter Wilson (Director)

"New stuff" in this context must be taken to mean stuff written over the last four years. I suppose. The only problem being that when they get around to reading the new stuff they'll be about four years behind.

To get back to the campaign of disruption and dislocation. It takes the form of intensifying the usual guerrilla activity—laughing behind my back, switching off the central heating after I've turned it on, a clever pretence of being deaf, cheering and shouting at television sport—all these are standard practice in our house. What's new is the Larky Practical Joke Done With Care and Love. For instance—when I sat down at my desk this morning, I noticed a large sheet of white paper in the centre, where the manuscript of the novel should have been. On it, in childish handwriting, was written:

Q: WHY DID THE LAVATORY ROLL?

And underneath this, in idiot capitals:

A: BECAUSE SOMEONE CAUGHT IT SHORT.
    Heh heh heh.
       Signed—The Black Phantom (Mrs)

Fair enough. I put it on one side and set about looking for the manuscript. I assumed she would have put it in the desk drawer. No luck. I went downstairs to the kitchen, where she was reading a cookery book and eating Weetabix straight from the packet.

"Ellen," I said, "what have you done with the manuscript?"

"What manuscript?" she said.

"My novel," I said.

"Oh," says Ellen, widening her eyes, and beginning to go into the Edvard Munch Scream facial, "are you writing a novel?"

"Not at the moment," I reply rather wittily, "at the moment I'm looking for a novel."

"There are plenty upstairs on the shelves," says Ellen. She wrinkles her nose, narrows her eyes and slides sideways in the chair. Then, suddenly, she stiffens, head up, like a gazelle smelling a leopard in the vicinity.

"*But*," she continues, "how will you know which is yours?"

She holds this last position (*Bad Doings At The Manor*) for some seconds. I return to the study.

Found it found it found it. So there. Quite nice though. In the drawer with her knickers. And, it occurs to me as I flick through the pages of the book, that a somewhat similar campaign to the one now being mounted against me, was mounted by me against Derek, all those years ago. Not straight away. After my unpleasant experience on the greensward I retreated to the river, didn't tell either Julie or Derek I'd seen them, returned home with Julie and carried on much as before. The fact is that I was, in those days, something of a voyeur and the sight of her screwing had only made Julie more desirable.

But, when I'd had time to think, and, when I'd stopped feeling like a cardboard box that had been left out in the rain, I got to work on Derek. The mission? To make his life as unbearable as possible, without causing physical injury. I contemplated all sorts of tortures. I was going to sell him shares in a South African goldmine and then expose him to the University Newspaper. I was going to enter him for *Opportunity Knocks*. I was going to dedicate countless records to him on Radio Luxembourg, under the pen name Mabel ("And now for Derek Sloman of Oxford from his wife Mabel. Mabel says she wants to thank you for being a wonderful husband for the last year. Every day and in every way he gets better and better, says Mabel.")

In fact, I only got one item in my portfolio of malice off the ground. This consisted of a letter to *Woman*. The letter was addressed to the problem page. It went:

Dear Evelyn Home,

I am writing to you (although I am a man) because I think you may be able to help me. My problem is this. I am afraid that my penis is pitifully small. I know this is said by many experts to be unimportant, but mine is really, *really* small. I have measured it several times and, even when erect, it only measures three inches long and about half an inch wide. What can I do about this? Please print my name and address as

40

I wish other sufferers to know that, awful as my problem is, I am not ashamed.

> Yours,
> Derek Sloman,
> Oxford

They didn't print all the letter, but they printed enough to matter. I left a copy of the magazine, open at the relevant page, in the Junior Common Room. Sensation in the Rugby team. A group of wags, one drunken night, set out to discover the true facts of the case. I watched from my window as, for the second time, Derek's trousers were lowered in my presence.

Fun as all this was, of course, it did no good at all. Julie liked going out with me, but, with her going out meant just that. I amused her. I knew about Books and Films. But she wasn't at all interested in going to bed with me, and, although she vaguely despised Derek, and was even prepared to bitch about him with me, she still liked fucking him. And, in my occasional moments of honesty, I had to admit to myself that what they had been doing in the wood was closer to Sex than I would ever get. I was so demoralised, I even stopped masturbating. The fact was—I wasn't goodlooking enough.

Am I getting maudlin in my old age? The poison ivy of the late twenties. Because, reading through all this stuff in the novel (most of it fairly mainstream comic), I find myself sadder than I thought. And more hopeless. When I come to read through what is supposed to be a serious transcription of how I felt at the time— jealousy of Derek, loneliness, insecurity, I don't know what   I find that doesn't convince me either. I can painfully put down exactly what I felt when I saw them together, or when we went out as a threesome and I *knew* Derek was screwing her, but it doesn't make any sense. I can't believe in the person I was then. That's frightening, isn't it? Nothing ties me to my past self except the mechanical act of my writing about it. It's like that awful feeling of unreality you get when reading a friend's private and personal diary (unknown to the friend). However closely the facts or the style correspond to your knowledge of that person, something, somewhere, is bound to be wrong'. Surely, you think, as you flick guiltily through the pages, no one can be as appallingly lacking in self-knowledge as this? But that isn't the point ... the point is that that *is* self-knowledge—a broken thing ...

I am getting maudlin in my old age. And the thing that strikes me most about the book (after its merits) is its sentimentality. There's a passage describing how I finally got the brush off from Julie. I'd tried, from time to time, to inject a little passion into our conversations about Chaucer or the Revolutionary Socialist Students' Federation and, up to this particular point, she'd always been quite nice about it. Without actually coming across of course. Then, one afternoon, when we were watching a Rugby match in which Derek was playing, I tried again and, in as nice a way as possible, she told me what I already knew. Now here is the curious thing. In the novel I've gone into everything she said, but, thinking about it now, what stands out in my mind is what happened *after* she'd finished talking.

There was nothing much I could do, of course, but watch the game. I couldn't walk away directly—too hang-dog. And I didn't think I'd be able to manage the face-to-face meeting with Derek afterwards. I planned to watch the match for about five minutes and then clear off. Focusing the attention on something, even if it was only thirty odd louts punching and kicking each other in a sea of mud, might stop the absurd pricking at the eyes, the sudden flush I felt in the face, combined with the sensation that Julie's words ("You see Derek and I are very ... *sexually* attracted and ...") had been piped into the homes of all my closest friends. Love, I thought to myself, is a way women have of keeping you guessing, a lie, a con-trick, a kick in the stomach, a—

As we watched, the confused tangle of bodies in the centre of the pitch started to writhe this way and that, like a sea monster giving birth. And, as the crowd (all fifteen of them) hallooed appreciation, parturition took place. From the belly of the monster emerged, plastered in mud, huger than ever before, Derek, clutching an oval ball. I had never realised before quite how big he was. Big even for a giant. He loped off through the drizzle towards the high white H at the other end of the ground. The only problem for Derek, really, as far as Rugby was concerned, was working out which end of the ground to run to. Once he'd got that sussed—it was no contest.

On this occasion, by some fluke, he must have got the right end, because other Rugby players, in different coloured shirts, were doing their level best to stop him in his tracks. Kamikaze-like, in insect squadrons, they threw themselves forward under his gigantic boots, only to be ground into the mud, along with their comrades. They tried to trip him up. They pinched. They bit. They clawed. They climbed up his back. They pulled his hair and generally behaved like irate tinies in a corporation playground. Hopeless. The scene resembled one of those fight sequences in a film with a prehistoric setting, in which men in skins, years ahead of their time, take on a brontosaurus without success. As Derek lumbered on it became apparent to me that nothing short of a landmine was going to stop him. It also became apparent to the opposing team who, gradually, gave up the attempt and stood around sneering to themselves, arms akimbo, as Derek headed off into the mist.

When he finally reached the line at the end of the pitch, he stopped and looked back, shyly. Behind him, strung out in the mud, twenty-nine weary faces watched him. Slowly, he stooped and deposited the ball just the other side of the line. A pause. Still no one moved. Then, as slowly, he stooped to pick it up again. Not until he was standing with the ball tucked under his arm like a Christmas present did the referee, wide-eyed and vacant-mouthed, blow a long, lonely blast on his whistle. The spectators, a long way behind everyone, applauded. "My God," I thought, as I turned to walk away, "you couldn't say I lost out to an ordinary man."

6

She is making a hell of a lot of noise this morning. I have a new suspicion. Just now she came in and stood by the door. She then held up a pair of my underpants and displayed them to an imaginary crowd, rather like a bullfighter giving the *aficionados* an eyeful of The Ears. She then left the room. I paid no attention. Later she returned with a bra and went through the same routine. Still I paid no attention. Now, however, Oswald (I'm pretty sure it was Oswald, coerced by Ellen) has pushed a note under my door. It reads:

WHAT DO YOU THINK WE'RE DOING ? (P.T.O.)

And, on the other side:

WE'RE PACKING!!!!

I suspect the whole thing is a veiled suggestion that I should go to the launderette. Oswald has an unhealthy obsession with the launderette. Often I watch him looking across at it from the pub, wistfully. He likes the friendly South London ladies who advise him (each time he goes) how to work the machines. Most of all he likes the time it takes. Twenty minutes to pack the bag, twenty minutes to find the necessary change, twenty minutes to find an empty machine and then an endless crossing and re-crossing from pub to launderette, to make sure that Things Are Still Going Round. It can take Oswald a whole day to wash three shirts and two pairs of underpants. Add to this the fact that he invariably, on returning from these expeditions, finds socks tucked behind paperbacks on the bookshelf and dirty shirts under his and my beds, and that he always loses at least four garments per trip, and you might well be forgiven for concluding that the simplest and cheapest way for Oswald to keep his clothes clean would be for him to make regular trips into the Menswear Department of Marks & Spencer. Actually—

I said I wasn't going to put Oswald in a novel. But God it is a temptation. I think it would be easier to resist if he and Ellen didn't keep interrupting me. I must get my head down and perhaps they won't try and involve me in the Launderette Problem. It's curious, actually, how much easier it is to write this journal than to work at the novel. The manuscript is at the other end of my desk, fat and neat. Maybe I feel I've done enough for the moment. I've earned a rest. I've earned the right to chew over my past, trying to make sense of it. Where was I?

Yes. I still continued seeing Derek and Julie after the Rugby match heart-to-heart, but I didn't see nearly so much of them. I was polite and distant. And, in the last term of my second year, they were married. I'll come to that later. The most important thing that happened to *me* in the meanwhile was that, having tried and failed to lose my virginity in this country, I reasoned, like many before me, that it might be easier abroad. And so, in the summer vacation, I took myself to Israel, land of students, oranges and opportunity, not to mention machine-guns. Needless to say, I went to a kibbutz, and it was there I had what I might term my Great Personal Rethink.

It was a lot of things. For a kickoff, I was sexually initiated by a large, enthusiastic corporal in the Israeli Army. A *girl*, don't worry. Together we picked fruit and made the two-backed beast. She was simple, uncomplicated and enormously demanding. When I wasn't rolling around with her I was playing communal games and/or singing Havanah Nagilah, a number I cannot hear to this day without getting severe cramp in my right leg. The kibbutz, whatever anyone else has said about it, is essentially a Jewish equivalent of Gordonstoun. The most unbearable feature of the place is the Youth, many of whom will do (almost) anything to get hold of a Rolling Stones record.

My moment of truth, however, was not inspired by dislike of

Jewish Nationalism or by hard physical work. It came, one hot afternoon in a field, when there was no one else but me and a guy called Avishai about. Avishai was a sort of village idiot with whom I had been set to work. Our job was to pick up discarded and broken fruit branches from the edges of this field, and, as the field was about two miles square, I spent practically my whole time in Israel trying to clean it. It was restful work, however, as Avishai and I spent most of our time flat on our backs eating oranges and discussing the world. Discussing the world with Avishai was, in many ways, harder than any other work I have ever known. He had only a limited command of his own language, Hebrew, and about three words of German. He added to this a sprinkling of English, picked up from people like myself in the long, hot summer afternoons.

There we were, anyway, Avishai sitting in the shade, looking out over the field, his hat well down over his eyes. Me, lying full length beside him. Suddenly, he shaded his eyes with his hand, like a Red Indian who has sighted the wagon train. I sat up as well, afraid that our Boss, who bore the quaint name of Gia-Ora, might be on his way. But nothing could I see. Just mile upon mile of fruit trees and pubescent vines stretching on and on towards the Dead Sea. I wrinkled my brows in unspoken question.

"Later," said Avishai, "we will become tractors."

"Really?" I said.

"Yes," said Avishai, "we become tractors."

"Terrific," I said.

"Then we become grapes, we become trailer, we become clippairs, we become also protective clothing."

"It's going to be a busy afternoon," I said.

Bekommen, of course, meant to get, didn't it? In German? Not for the first time, I reflected on the absurdity of the English going abroad to seek Experience. Given the English social system, it could only be a way of confirming one's prejudices. There were so many things one could become (not in Avishai's sense) and they were all pre-ordained. If you lived abroad and married a foreign girl and learned the language, impossible to escape one's background. The English have a word for it, "going native".

46

What can you do against a language like that?

And that language difficulty, I thought to myself as Avishai grinned down at me, wasn't only to do with words. It was the heart of the mess I was in, part of the reason why I felt helplessly programmed towards failure. Feeling things always at the wrong time, loving people too early or too late, always being hurt by or despising girls, never quite getting it right. And, it occurred to me—half the mistakes I'd made with Julie were self-willed, deliberate, part of the same eager progress towards misery. They arose out of looking for something—call it love if you like—and going on asking for it even when I didn't find exactly that commodity in stock. What had I wanted to feel about Julie? Feelings that went with a particular kind of autumn evening— kisses in the damp outdoors and so on ... and I had gone on hammering away at the front door, asking her for those things, when I should have realised long ago I was the wrong customer at the wrong shop. Now with Refka (my Israeli corporal) I was the right customer at the right shop only because I hadn't asked her for anything. Being a foreigner. Maybe I'd never be able to ask anything of anyone. Like those guys you read about who'd masturbated so much they could never have normal sex. You could blame Julie for all that—or rather blame Julie for being around at just the wrong time in my life.

"This," said Avishai, chewing a piece of grass, "is good arbeit."

"You," I said in a friendly tone, "are a boring, work-shy, repetitive cretin."

"Yes," said Avishai, "good."

Travel, I thought to myself—how it broadens the mind. I gave myself up to the fantasy that Avishai and I were actually *becoming* tractors, wheels sprouting where our arms used to be and bright red steel bodies instead of arms and legs. And why, to continue my earlier train of thought, should I not change myself, not jolt off the rails of predestination towards a new identity? Being English and middle class I could not escape, but I could escape being English and middle class and defeated. I've always believed, actually, that that is what "maturity" is—not a

47

deepening and a broadening of the personality but a series of cheap tricks designed to cope with one's (essentially) unalterable circumstances. Lying there beside Avishai, reviewing my behaviour at the wedding and my total failure to surmount the Julie thing, I evolved, quite coldbloodedly, a plan of campaign.

The problem facing me, really, was this:

1. I needed a great love affair BUT
2. I had become aware that "love" is in fact a con-trick SO
3. It was important to forget 2 in any search for 1 and 1 in any search for 2.

In other words—if I was going to get to screw Julie I would have to assume that I did not love her. Once I had assumed that I would be able to behave as if I *did* love her or as if I *didn't* as the occasion demanded. And this gave me a possible psychological advantage over her. Because she would never be quite sure whether I was serious or not, whereas I would always know that I was *not* serious even when I was serious. To put it crudely, it occurred to me out there in that field, flanked by Avishai and watching the flies snap and circle by the hedge, that, to get anywhere in this life, I was going to have to be a little bit of a monster. But a lovable monster, a monster *malgré lui*.

I've jumped ahead a little. One of the things that led me to this position must have been the wedding and the way I behaved after it. I blew it very badly at the wedding itself. I'd almost decided not to go. They held it in the College Chapel one hot afternoon. I can remember Julie now, pencil-nosed, livid of complexion, and wearing, rather implausibly, white. And me at the back of the church, by myself in my only smart suit. I kept having this fantasy that Derek would be unable to remember the responses and that men would be hired to conceal themselves around the altar. At the crucial moment, they would hold up large cards on which would be written things like:

"I DO."

Nothing of this nature happened. They were a credit to each other. And afterwards she leaned on his elbow and craned her neck up to look at him and generally looked the perfect picture of the bride. I suppose anyone with a modicum of talent for acting doesn't find it difficult to look convincing at their wedding, and Julie had more than a modicum of talent. I got astoundingly drunk with a wag called Minton. In the middle of the reception she came up to me (by this time she was drunk and her headdress or whatever they call it was over her left eye). She said, giving me the snaggle-toothed smile:

"It was fun wasn't it?"

Then her face bunched up and her eyes shone. She looked like Mrs Hamster House-Proud in a particularly badly drawn children's book.

"What was?" I asked.

"Everything."

"Julie," I said, "you have the biggest capacity for self-deception of anyone I know."

"Yes," she said. "Yes." And her little hamster eyes beamed enthusiastically.

"Julie," I continued, swaying slightly under the influence of half a bottle of Bollinger, "you are marrying a man whose only distinction is that he is over seven feet tall. You are marrying a man without any trace of imagination or sensitivity. I would rather, Julie, watch religious programmes on T.V. than spend half an hour with your husband. He is a kind of student Man Mountain, Julie. He will break the bed, Julie—people should be insured against the possibility of meeting your husband." I said much more in the same vein. Julie listened to me, smiling drunkenly, and when I'd finally ground to a halt she put her hand on my arm.

"I know," she said, "but it was fun wasn't it?"

"Yes," I said. And, in spite of myself, I smiled back at her, wondering how someone could look like Mrs Hamster House-Proud and Lucrezia Borgia at one and the same time.

I blew even more cool when they moved into their house, a bijou residence in Summertown—the *Radio Times* and *T.V. Times* in a blue folder on the television, small glass animals (belonging to Derek) on the mantelpiece, and a pair of the biggest slippers I have ever seen in my life over by the curtains. I sent a card to their home address. On it was a picture of a golden labrador, and, over the labrador, was written "Welcome On Your First Day In Your New Home! Love from Gladys." I lay in wait for Julie outside the Bodleian one evening, and, when she asked me, coyly:

"Who's Gladys?"

I replied:

"Gladys was the dog on the front."

Julie looked up at me with the new wife and mother look she'd developed from the day before the wedding. A blank. There were many more such disastrous attempts at humour or bravery, whichever you want to call it, but it was picking at the scab, thinking how to talk myself into her charmed circle that brought me to the pitch of desperation. I'd tried all the better but sincere tricks. I was led inevitably to Israel, that field, Avishai and my Big Personal Rethink. A true moment of insight—from man to monster in a quarter of an hour.

I still don't feel like working at the novel. Curious.

Lunch soon. Wonder what it'll be? The packing joke has
continued, possibly to the exclusion of lunch and certainly to the
exclusion of serious thought about the Novel. They were doing
Nautical Loading a moment ago, which went something like this:

Ellen (on my landing):	Aye aye up there!
Oswald (in the hall):	Aye aye up there!
Ellen (basso profondo):	Cargo ahoy!
Oswald:	What cargo have you?
Ellen:	A suitcase.
Oswald:	Avast there my hearties!

(Ellen switches to a stage whisper, easily audible by me)

Ellen:	What if they find out I'm a girl?
Me:	THEY'LL RAPE YOU!!!

(Silence. My joke has fallen flat.) After a while, Oswald starts to
sing a song. It goes:

OSWALD'S SONG

With a ro and a re and a ro lo ro
And a hi tiddle hi cockalorum.
We pack and we sow and we're very very low
At six at six
At six at six
At six o'clock in the morning.

After Oswald had given us several verses of this song, he and
Ellen evolved a kind of chorus, which went:

Aye aye up there!
The boat's in!
Aye aye! Aye aye!

There was then a very, very long pause, at the end of which Oswald came in, with a newly developed high falsetto screech. He sounded like Alfred Deller stuck on a barbed wire fence. The chorus postlude went:

> *Tooo* the greenwood, *tooo* the greenwood
> *Tooo* the greenwood, greenwood tree.

This was repeated *da capo al fine* until I went to the door and screamed at them to shut up. There was then total, deafening silence for about a minute, then, again, very close to the door I heard Ellen whisper—"He is angry!" For this she had adopted a Historico-rustic accent. Oswald too went briefly Mummerset for the next dialogue:

Oswald:	He is a great lord. A writer they say.
Ellen:	Let us away.
Oswald:	Aye. Let us. But whither?
Ellen:	Leeds.
Oswald:	Leeds?
Ellen:	Aye. Leeds.

More scampering. Oswald does a quick ascent and descent of stairs. Ellen has been suspiciously quiet. As silence settles once again, my past self shivers into life, detaches itself from the page like a transfer peeling off one's skin, leaving half itself behind. Me then.

After I got back from Israel, I spent two or three weeks at a friend's house in the Lake District working out a plan of campaign. I also wrote several brief pieces which I entitled "Essays On Human Relationships". Most of these, thank God, I have thrown away, but I can remember enough of them to put together an imitation of one. I'd like to find a way of using it in the book—but at the moment the plot is so tight I can't see a way of working it in. That's the problem with having a narrator figure. But, if you're writing a book with *style*, I suppose you have to sacrifice incident.

RULES FOR JULIE

Number one rule of seduction is:

Forget your own fantasy. There is not room in any relationship for both partners to imagine they are getting what they want. From forgetting this basic rule came all my first mistakes with Julie. I must now ditch any idea of fulfilling any of my fantasies, romantically speaking, so that I may be at liberty to examine Julie in the objective fashion essential to any prospective lover.

WHAT DOES JULIE WANT?

Answer: it depends on who she imagines she is. The most important thing about her is that she lives, almost exclusively, in a world of fantasy. Her whole behaviour since The Marriage has been like a clever parody of domesticity.

Now, apart from her fantasy life, Julie is an essentially commonplace woman. As far as I can see her romantic life has gone Harris, Me, Derek, and we can presume that, insofar as it existed before that, it followed the same pattern, i.e. Great Lover to Talk To and Fuck followed by Good Friend to Talk Things Over With followed by Reliable Chap to Fuck Pure and Simple. Which means that she is now ready for a Great Lover. And IT DOESN'T REALLY MATTER WHO THIS IS!! If it isn't me it could be a North Oxford milkman so it better be me. The important thing is the categories rather than the people who fulfil them. What I have to do is to get an idea of what Julie's idea of an extra-marital fuck might be. Write and ask her?

Does she want a yob?

A genius?

Another woman perhaps?

I wrote several theses around this topic, and finally came up with a persona that I thought suitable. I decided that, most of all, Julie wanted to feel safe, and that the perfect personality was that of a broken-down family friend, a kind of Dobbin. This rôle meant that I didn't have to alter much, since, previously, I think I had been the only one of the threesome not under the illusion that I was a Dobbin-style family friend. It also chimed in with Julie's new desire to be an Earth Mother figure.

I did a very thorough job. Bearing in mind the fact that Julie had never trusted me, I needed a convincing off-stage event to account for my new view of myself. I went through the motions of having a minor nervous breakdown and spent three pleasant weeks in the Warneford Hospital, being visited by a long string of earnestly sympathetic college friends.

I telephoned the Warneford late one night from a coin-box telephone in the College—a woman answered.

"Look," I said, "I think I ought to come along and see you."

"Yes," said the woman, "appointments, appointments are—"

"No," I said, "now."

"Listen—"

"Now. Is that O.K.?"

She thought about it and then decided to behave as if the request hadn't been made.

"Appointments are—"

I put the phone down and went out into the High and watched the last few people totter home, and red and black Oxford buses tear past on their way to Blackbird Leys or Cowley. Then I went back and dialled the number again.

"Hullo, Warneford Hospital!"

"Hullo. It's me again."

"Listen—" said the woman.

"If you don't let me in I just thought you might like to know I'm going to jump off the top of the Bodleian Library."

A wary pause.

"Well, we can't have that, can we?"

"It's up to you," I said.

In the tone of someone who knows they are being conned but is too bored to do anything about it, she replied:

"Do you know where we are?"

"You bet," I said, "keep a cell warm."

The doctor who interviewed me was called Schwarz. He wore

a white coat, but that was about the closest he got to medical science; our two sessions mainly consisted of a pause. The pause would begin as embarrassing, ripen into a sort of significance, stretch into mere dullness and then sharpen into excruciating agony while Schwarz tapped his pencil on the desk. Then he'd say something like:

"What do you think's wrong with you?"

"I don't know," I'd reply, "I thought you were supposed to be the psychiatrist."

Then it was back to the pause, with me looking out of the window. We did get into the early life/bedwetting bit at one stage, but my answers were so plainly facetious that even Schwarz saw the futility of the exercise. After the second session, he gave me a large bottle of anti-depressant tablets, red in colour, which, I was informed, would kill me if I ate broad beans or Marmite with them. I saw patients rushing out of the Warneford, along to the Supermarket, picking up a loaf, a jar of Marmite and a can of broad beans and spreading on the pills greedily—wham bam suicide butty.

After a while he left me alone—which was what I wanted in the first place.

Finally, two days before I was released, Julie turned up. I can remember her now wearing the brown levis with the paint marks on the left leg, and her hair scraped back across her forehead in a very grown-up way. She looked like a posh Madonna, there was something of the fashion model about her. I gave her the new line. I told her my previous attempts at hardness, cynicism and sharpness were a pose I felt no longer able to sustain. I always knew, I told her, that Derek was the right person for her. I even said, finding it difficult to choke back the laughter as I did, that one day I hoped to have someone of my own. I would just have to keep waiting.

To my surprise she leaned forward across the bed (for some ludicrous reason I had chosen to remain in bed for the interview) and took my hand. She looked deep into my eyes, and said: "Don't *worry*, love. I understand." Did I notice then that edge to the glance, the sweep away to the floor from me, or the hint of

55

narrowness in the way she watched me as she turned to say good-bye? I don't think so. I was intoxicated with what I took to be success, and all I could think about was the fact that she and Derek had invited me to dinner the following Thursday. Jules et Jim. I'd give them Jules et Jim.

When Thursday came, I had my second-stage plan well worked out. I took a bus up to Summertown and, at eight o'clock, the three of us were sitting down to one of Julie's newly-wed meals. Tinned soup, meat and veg, followed by large helpings of pie. I waited for the third course before making my move....

"The league prospects," said Derek, "are a bleeding sight worse than—a bigger helping of pie, please."

"*There* we are!" said Julie.

"With cream," said Derek.

"*There*," she said again.

"I mean what are they doing? What *are* they doing? Sugar thanks please."

"I think it's bad," I said cautiously (I hadn't been studying football very long), "but I mean I don't know *how* bad you know ..."

I let this sentence trail away into silence. No one offered to fill the silence. In a panic I said:

"I mean it's not as bad as last year, right?"

Julie looked at me. It was not part of the rules, really, for her to suspect me of taking the piss. In Julie's book, the people who tried to make fun of her or anything connected with her, were, by definition, insecure and hopeless, and, although I had recently come on as precisely those things, I wasn't enough of a deadbeat to be suspected of the worst crime of all—Not Taking Her Seriously. She smiled a wifely smile and said, in the Dingley Dell voice:

"Pie?"

"Mmm," I replied, tucking my chair under the table, "pie. Lovely."

The three of us began to eat. Derek champing slowly, Julie in the newly-acquired ladylike fashion and me in my "intellectual" manner, i.e. a mouthful followed immediately by a sentence.

56

However intellectually I ate, though, I could not rid myself of the impression that we were not in North Oxford at all, but miles below ground in Mr Badger's lair—the seats little, mossy toadstools and the knives and forks blades of grass. I watched them both carefully, waiting for just the right moment to make my request.

"Did you see the United game?" said Derek, after one of the longest pauses in dinner-party history.

"Yeah," I said, eating in double quick time in the hope that this might provide a reasonable imitation of excitement, "it was a nice one."

"The defence," said Derek, "they should shoot the whole of the fucking defence."

"Right," I said, wondering, if there was any danger of the conversation becoming more specific—something in the nature of a direct factual question, possibly about the rules of the game, from Derek to me . . . Luckily, just thinking about the defence was enough to set Derek back to his piece of pie.

What did they talk about, I wonder, when I wasn't there? Did Derek swagger in and swap jokes in French? Was he a different man? That question still puzzles me, even now, all these years later. I imagine him walking in from the Bodleian, dropping his books on the sofa and staggering across to the telly. Appalling to think that there are probably still students who refuse to conform to the stereotype of being idle, drunk and/or anarchic. To get back to me at the dinner party finally making my move. . . .

"I wondered," I said, when I judged the time was right, "I wondered whether I could ask you both something."

"Ask away," said Derek, genial host to this Joint Decision.

"I wondered . . . I mean . . . I know it's an awful imposition but I wondered what the sort of . . . room situation might be here."

I said this in my I'm-hopeless-but-lovable way. The feeling I intended to evoke was a combination of pity, trust and contempt. All of these three emotions in her face, Julie said:

"Aren't things working out with Anna?"

To complete my new persona, I had invented a girlfriend called Anna. I had told Julie all about her at the Warneford.

57

Anna was horse-faced, kind and practical. She read Geography at St Hilda's. She had sexual problems. Talking about her to Julie, I held a clear picture of her in my mind and then talked as if I were really fond of her. The information got across just the same. It amused me to watch her deciding what kind of person Anna was and then setting about the task of incorporating her into her oh-so-cosy and radiant universe. The ecstasy of the private joke was in describing her appearance minutely, dwelling on the details of her routine ("She works pretty late most nights—in the College library." "She cuts her own hair." Etc, etc.) and watching Julie, flushed with superiority and warmth, say things like: "Oh Martin, she sounds *just* the girl for you."

The curious thing was, I remember thinking as Julie smiled sympathy across the table, how terribly easy it could be to conform to other people's idea of you—easier than taking the trouble of carving out a personality for yourself. If I went on at this rate no woman in England would be Martin-proof.

"Didn't things work out?" said Julie.

I re-arranged my face into the crumpled clown expression and said:

"She's ... met another guy."

"Really?"

"Yeah."

A brave little smile. Derek cut himself another piece of pie, well into four figures, calorie-wise. Was ordinary food enough for him? Would he start on the crockery next?

"Yeah—he's ... a real flash character."

"How do you mean?"

"Oh you know ... incredibly good at sport and so on."

A tide of private hilarity rose in my throat. That was brilliant—"sport"—just the right tone of shut-out school-boyness. At the mention of the word, Derek applied the air brakes to his jaws and slowed his calorie intake to a mere 750 per second. Julie leaned forward and fingered the tablecloth. In her new rôle as wife and mother, she had to be sympathetic.

"Is he at the University?"

"No," I said, "he's a computer programmer."

58

Once again, a muffled snort of glee rose within me. I felt the familiar pleasure (at least familiar since the post-kibbutz Rethink) of feeling that a third person was always present, for whose benefit I was acting out an immensely entertaining charade. Julie wavered, smiled, and bought it.

"If you need a place," she said, "we've always got room. Haven't we, Derek?"

"Mmmgraiouw," said Derek, through his piece of pie. In the bag, I thought. In the bleeding bag.

Does my past self seem just a little on the odious side? It's worth thinking about. In mitigation it should be argued that I hadn't exactly had the breaks to enable me to be a nice guy. And being a nice guy is, after all, only another, subtler way of getting what you want. All of the real shits I've ever known have been recognised everywhere as "nice". I'd adopted the distant, jokey tone I thought suitable to girls and it hadn't worked. What could I do but try something else? All this is important for the novel. Because, when the chips are down, I'm not concerned to give a "fair and rounded" picture of me. I want to get some of that hatred and arrogance into the story because that is how I felt, and in fact I think I was right to feel that. Do not go gentle out of that bad girl. How else was I supposed to lay the fantasy of romantic love except by another fantasy—this time the fantasy of revenge? I'm afraid I could not, *cannot* forget and move on to other things. I went back over those afternoons spent in her rooms in Bardwell Road, the time at the ball when she talked about Harris, the lies she had told me outside cinemas in the north and the south of the city of Oxford. I went back over all these things in my mind, as I do now in this room, and, while remaining a normal youth, I became, like so many of us if you slice our motives open, slightly barmy, one-tracked on an emotion that ought to have been part of growing up. I had and hold to all of that—she shall not be spared.

What about Julie as Fictional Character though? I can hear the critics ask. How can you give credibility to someone you hate? What about her Motives? Hasn't she any Normal Human Emotions? Well, I suppose she had, but I can't make that matter

59

to me and it will not matter to my hero. It doesn't matter a *fuck* that she was probably miserable and scared, and looked at me and thought "Jesus—this bloke is (a) ugly and (b) dangerous". The fact of the matter is that she hurt me and how can I disentangle that from the memories I have of her? I was afraid of her then, that too colours my picture of her now. I want her to open the first page of this novel and see herself described and then turn, hurriedly, to the next chapter and see more of herself described, and then say "well at least it's no good" and then read more and be forced to admit against her will that it *is* good because it's cruel, as cruel as she was to me all those years ago. A just payment.

I don't go for all this Greek tragedy shit anyway. It would be possible to go over what I've written and slip in a few paragraphs about her point of view. I'm sure, for instance, in that scene by the river, that I've put into the novel almost straight, I could provide a reasonable imitation of her train of thought that might even earn me phrases like "Mr Steel's understanding of women is remarkable in one so young." You know the kind of thing?

". . . She looked across at Stephen. He pushed his glasses back on to his nose and started to uncork the wine. It was like being driven, she thought. Sometimes you sat in the car and moved from A to B without thinking, and, at other times, you spent your whole time jerking and shuddering and braking and wondering how anyone ever got anywhere on wheels. They had to go through the learner driver phase but please God they learned on someone else.

"She lay full length on the grass. He really was awfully sweet. But . . ."

And so on. You see I don't deny that she had her point of view and her tragedy. In fact when you tot up me, Harris and Derek, I think she had more than her fair share, but in the novel I am not concerned with the Mature View. And, also, I do not hold with the literary convention that demands that the author "understands" his characters. In real life one comes across people whom one loathes, why shouldn't you write about people you loathe? Imagine a sensitive modern novel about Hitler.

Just as in politics there are guilty parties, so it is in love. Once again I move away from the book (am I getting bored with it?) and back to me moving into their house with my caseful of paperbacks and dirty underpants, sellotaping my picture of Bob Dylan onto my bedroom wall, sniffing out the local pub, and lying in bed, giggling to myself at my own cleverness. I want to go back over those first few weeks, as the seduction plan moved smoothly into gear. I want to re-live my days as a backdoor man.

But before I do, I must eat. There hasn't been a peep out of Oswald or Ellen for ages. Maybe I will go to the launderette. I need a break from my past. Why *should* it be so difficult to make sense of it?

8

3.00 p.m.

A strange one. I've just returned from a tour of the house. Oswald and Ellen are nowhere to be seen. And, by the stove in the kitchen, I found a plate on which was a pork chop (lukewarm) and some baked beans. The kitchen, by the way, was originally planned as "the heart of the house". Ellen said she was going for something "relaxed and peasanty", and, in furtherance of this aim, bought hundreds of small cupboards, mostly of pinewood, artificially aged, at great expense. It now looks like a museum re-creation of a Victorian slum. To return to the pork chop. Next to it was a piece of paper with a crudely drawn arrow pointing towards it, and by the arrow was written the word "LUNCH". On the pork chop was a cocktail stick with a little white flag on top, and, on the flag was written a two line poem, which said:

> Eat the pork and then the beans,
> That is what this message means!

Just to cap all of this, next to the kettle I found a thick envelope, sealed with wax, and addressed to me in Ellen's Joke Spinster handwriting. In the top left-hand corner it said "By Hand. To be opened after my death or on December 25th, whichever is the sooner. E. Steel." I know what's in it—a cartoon or a dead frog or something. I think perhaps that communication between Ellen and myself has finally broken down. I have put the letter and my lunch on the desk, next to the manuscript of the novel. The fact of the matter is—I'm getting a little bored with these jokes. I think that, after I've finished the novel, Ellen and I should sit down and ask each other whether there is anything between us apart from an elaborate series of gags. Perhaps, like Morecambe and Wise, we should find different partners and only meet when the needs of showbiz beckon. In a way, I suppose we construct games for each other and both enjoy playing them, but I think that this particular game has gone far enough. In concentrating on what I want to do I will have to leave her behind, even if only symbolically. And it is rather significant that this latest in a long line of wacky messages is the first one I haven't actually bothered to open. I can't be doing with any part of her personality in the room with me. Does this mean I don't love her? It certainly does mean that if I'm successful I might be leaving her behind.

I don't mean all of this. We get on fine really, but although I don't mean it, I did just think it. And so it does mark a turning point in my relationship with Ellen. In any relationship, the working day, as it were, is made up of thousands of decisions, changes of policy and so on, most of them not at all significant. But all those tiny changes, at the end of the day add up to something—you see a particularly hated gesture just once too often or, perhaps, write something down that you should have only thought. I remember someone telling me once of a couple who had been married very happily for ten years. Then, one afternoon, when they were shopping in Piccadilly, the husband crossed the road ahead of his wife. He was walking about two yards in front of her, and, suddenly, he placed his hand on his right buttock, inserted his first three fingers in the cloth-covered crevice of his behind and worked them round and round in a thorough gesture that obviously gave him great pleasure. She said later, after the divorce, that it was at that particular moment that she had fallen out of love with him. Great things can hang on a scratch at the bum.

Now I'm not saying that that letter from Ellen is the final straw. It is possible, anyway, that, like that lady, it is simply offering me an excuse. I don't even know yet that it *is* offering me an excuse, but I do know that the change I have gone through, the alteration in my feelings for Ellen, is as definite and final as an

63

alteration in the seasons. I suppose I'd better work out exactly what that change is.

Put it this way. Ellen and I are very secure with each other. We share an enormous number of jokes and experiences, which leads us to take liberties with each other. Now—I take fewer liberties with her because she has less to protect. That sounds conceited. All of this sounds complacent and conceited, but anyone's thoughts about themselves sound complacent when written down. I have to protect my work, not only from the hordes of philistines who run our publishing, television and theatre companies, but also from her. If Home Confidence slips, then I'm finished. She throws me over and finds a guy who has had the cunning not to let anyone know he Wants To Write. Her games, letters and jokes are each fresh attacks on my precarious dignity. And I feel enough of my dignity has been lost this morning. When she and Oswald return from wherever they've gone, I will deliver a short, Canute-style lecture, and the dialectic of our marriage will start again—Me purposeful, Her subversive, but, somehow, keeping the thing in balance.

Glad I cleared the air on that one. It's always best to be the first to move, in both romantic and military matters. With that decision behind me, I can return to Oxford, Summertown and those weeks I spent with Julie and Derek. Thank God I now *think* before saying anything to my woman of the moment. Sexual relations are, after all, a knack, not a gift from God. With Julie and Derek, I was still at the knack-learning stage, which, I suppose, gives the closing weeks of our relationship not the spuriousness of tragedy (i.e. everyone is doing their best and screwing each other up in the process) but the genuine awfulness of real life (i.e. everyone is trying to do everyone else down, but, in the process, screwing themselves up as well).

The awful thing was that I actually got to like Derek. I'd never really disliked him, except in his capacity as rival, and, living close to him, I grew to appreciate his finer qualities. I, also, quite involuntarily, grew to like football. Derek and I went to see Oxford United every Saturday (Reserves when they were playing away) and, three evenings a week we played bar billiards in the Gardener's Arms, just off the Banbury Road. Who was the fellow who said that you must be very careful about what you pretend to be, or you may end up becoming it? He said it better than that but that is what he meant, and little by little I began living the part of the slightly spare, eager to please, friend to all. Good Old Mart. It wasn't that difficult. "Oh *nice* one," as Derek clocked up another three thousand break, and I, once again, failed to score more than ten. "Do me a *favour*," as the Oxford United mid-field cripples staggered through another ritual humiliation, letting some unknown Third Division team clock up goal after goal with terrifying ease and speed.

The effect of all this was, inevitably, to put Julie out into the cold. For Derek, although he improved on acquaintance, was without doubt what Ellen would call a male chauvinist, i.e. a slob to women. He did tend to sit, knife and fork in hand, awaiting his three-course meal, discussing the finer points of last Saturday's game with me, while Julie smiled and bobbed between kitchen and sitting-room. I wasn't sure whether the nightly moans and screams of ecstasy coming from their bedroom quite compensated for this. Actually, I came to relish their love bouts as pieces of impromptu theatre—the steady thump of the bed-head, the slow crescendo of grunts from Derek, and Julie giving, on every conceivable occasion, the performance of a lifetime. "Moans and screams of ecstasy" doesn't really do it justice. It started rather like the wind in distant telephone wires, and, over twenty minutes worked up to the Ride of the Valkyries plus Steam Hammer and Landslide. But, strange are the ways of nature. With Derek on tap, as it were, Julie naturally became more interested in me, the qualities of my mind and my way with the cutting epigram (see Harris). Though I say it myself, I played it brilliantly, or, to be more precise, I thought I was playing it brilliantly. I didn't give her an inch. The more she wanted to talk about Kafka and the eighteenth-century novel, the more obsessed I appeared to become with billiards and league tables. Thinking about it now of course, I—but things must be put down in their proper place.

The only drawback, it seemed to me, of my master plan was

the fact that I was becoming quite incredibly fat. Derek needed at least thirteen pints of Double Diamond per day in order to keep his system ticking over, and he shed this in bouts of Rugby, boxing, cross-country running and fucking. I, however, moved from pub to meal to bed, with no available form of exercise except self-abuse. In the middle of week three I altered my behaviour pattern. I maintained my friendly relations with Derek, but I started to hold long, intense conversations with Julie in the front room of their house. In these conversations I took the line that Derek was "Unique but Difficult". It was a superb strategy, since no one, not even his mother, had ever thought of Derek as Unique, and so this opened the way for a wholesale character assassination on my part. I went into his eating habits, his arguing ability, everything I could throw at him, all done in the "You know the amazing thing about old Derek *is* . . ." style. I did a pretty good impression of a man discovering the faults of his best friend and taking them to be virtues. Julie had to sit and take it. Because we were both in the house, presenting her with a unified masculine front, the only way for her to escape being a stooge was to separate us into Lover and Husband. Thus I reasoned, in my skilful, but not quite skilful enough, way.

I wonder where they've gone. Probably to Harrods, it being a Saturday. Oswald usually runs out of money at around three forty-five on Friday afternoon, and his weekends, when not spent in the launderette, are passed in a frantic search for fivers. He has a comprehensive knowledge of out-of-hours banking facilities, and his favourite is Harrods Bank, where he can be seen every Saturday at four thirty, alongside Norwegians, Americans and chronically inefficient other Britons. Ellen will have gone along with him because her second favourite place (after bed) is Harrods food store. She enjoys sneering at the bourgeoisie as they pick out exotic delicacies for their exotic little dinner parties. The thing I really hate about Oswald and Ellen is that they are so bloody *real*. I can't even make Julie and Derek, who are I suppose real people seen at a distance, do things quite the way they do.

The other week, for instance, I woke at four in the morning to hear a terrific noise in my left ear, rather like the crackling of plaster breaking up. I looked around for the damage, and after a while, made out in the darkness, Ellen's jaws, moving slowly and rhythmically. There was a long, suspense-movie-like pause, and then I said:

"Ellen."

"Yes," she said.

"Ellen," I said, "are you eating?"

"Yes," she said.

"What are you eating?" I asked.

"Ryvita," she replied. There was another long pause and then she added "And *cheese*." Then she laughed madly to herself. Now I'm not saying that I want Julie and Derek to do things like that, but I am saying that I find the process of turning them into fictional people difficult. The best bits of the novel, I think, are the things done straight from life, the moments I have preserved perfectly in my memory; but when the time comes for the people in these word-pictures of mine to get up, to move from room to room, to catch buses and trains, to say typical or untypical things, something happens to them and their movements become stiff and awkward. I'm not worried about this. I know with work I'll get it right, because I know that I can tell a story, but perhaps that is the reason why I use this journal for the secret, shameful pleasure of telling nothing but the truth.

More pictures of me and Derek and Julie. Standing at a door in her apron and smiling like a housewife in an advert. At a party, given by a girl in Northmoor Road, dancing by herself, playing cat's cradle with invisible string, hips grinding out the rhythm of the song. Why, I don't know, but another picture of me, Julie and Derek in a pub, although which pub and where I cannot remember. The picture fades, goes ragged at the edges, like a faulty television image, and, after the picture has gone there is nothing but silence. Derek doesn't move any more. Julie's smile, perhaps, is the last to go—with her eyes, ears, and nose turning to static round that tight, prissy little mouth. The image wavers. Julie is going. Back to cook the dinner. Derek and I are alone at the table, out-of-focus figures in the background; between us

67

there seems to be a comfortable silence; when our voices come, they are small and far-away.

"What'll you have?"

"Double Diamond," says Derek.

"Double Diamond it is."

I move up to the bar. I sneak a glance at Derek as I do so. He is staring into space, drumming his fingers on the table top. Waiting for his drink. Is this how Julie feels when she's feeding him? I think. That helpless, duty-inspired affection.

Let's face it—Derek needed me. He needed the comfortable phrases, the carefully protected image of masculinity that his less clever friends were unable to sustain. Chained by their various women—nurses, geographers, trainee teachers, secretaries, all part of a monstrous regiment of well-coordinated homemakers— Derek's old Rugby Club friends no longer had the romance of the saloon bar about them. He needed clever magicians like me to re-create the mood of his bachelor days. More pictures . . .

We are on a bus going north. There is a girl in the front seat. Otherwise, only Derek and I. She is sitting in the front seat of the bus, her black p.v.c. mac riding up over her thighs. Derek looks at her in blank incuriosity. Then his eyes move back to mine. When our glances meet, Derek's eyes brighten in an adequate imitation of lust.

"Not *bad*!" he says. "Not at *all* bad."

Julie, Derek and I are walking in Port Meadow, long, level, misty, the lights of the city visible in the distance. "It floods sometimes doesn't it?" says Julie. Derek and I walk on. Maybe there's a dog there. People's breath is in white clouds.

The three of us are at the cinema, watching a film by Ingmar Bergman. A vicar says to his lover, in Swedish "I loathe you." "Why?" she replies, also in Swedish. He replies with a long list, including, among other things, halitosis and eczema—all in Swedish. She stares back dully. Julie and I piss ourselves laughing. Derek smiles slowly, happy that his friends are enjoying themselves.

Then the three of us are on the river. Derek is punting, although it's cold. Perhaps we nicked the punt from somewhere.

68

Julie sits next to me. As we round a corner, the boat rocks, Julie falls against me and I put my arm on hers. We look at each other. Then we look up at Derek. Just for a second, he looks lost and miserable and hurt. Then he grins, picks up the punt-pole and drives it deep into the water. Everybody grins. There are more moments like this.

9

Which brings me to the last afternoon. *When* I use it in the book I don't know. At the moment the Stephen character and the based-on-Julie character are getting on embarrassingly well. My narrator figure went into quite a neat, if unpleasant speech about how ludicrous Stephen Jarrett and Sue Faversham looked together, that rather took me off the track. Is this why I've stopped after that initial twenty-thousand-word burst? I don't know. It's true that I've spent a lot of time asking myself questions about my narrator figure. How old is he? What are his politics? Is *he* a writer? (Terribly hack idea.) And so on. And yet I don't want to delineate him or my Julie/Derek/Me characters too clearly. I have to bleed just enough life out of my past to give it the weight of a symbol, in other words I have to *subtract* from reality, concentrate it. For instance, I have a scene where Stephen meets Sue in a pub. Now I don't think it need be a pub. I don't think we need to know exactly where they met. I think my narrator should get down to the essentials—the looks, the lies, the evasions . . . Rewrite the scene? It's very early days. We're just at the point where the Derek character, Roger Beamish, is about to lumber in—so maybe its being over-sweet is good.

Getting back to that afternoon—what do I feel about it? I was very sure a minute ago, but now as I come to write it down I'm not so sure. Was it in February? I do know that it was one of those cold, rainy days that starts late and finishes early and you think to yourself that maybe it should never have bothered in the first place.

She was sitting at the table in the kitchen, forehead propped on her hand. In front of her was a copy of *Gulliver's Travels*. It was warm in the kitchen and the light, already on at half past four, was cosily yellow, pleasantly nostalgic. I closed the door behind me, far too softly. She looked up.

"Hullo you!"

"Hi! I got bored," I said, moving into the room.

"Work's awful, isn't it?"

"Mmm."

There was another one of the pauses we'd started experiencing, in which, suddenly, the space between us expanded to several hundred miles and then zoomed down to a nose-to-nose six inches, as if space were a piece of elastic and someone had let go the other end. The odd thing about these pauses was that they weren't totally pleasant. There was a nasty air of anything-might-happen about them, a feeling that one of us was about to take a great risk or make a staggeringly awful mistake.

"Well," I said.

That only made the pause worse. The other awful thing was that I didn't have a manner to cope with this situation—indeed, of late I found I was running out of techniques of coping. This didn't apply to things like pantomime indecision, or naïveté when Derek said something embarrassing. I'd been doing those for so long and so well that Derek (and others) genuinely thought of me as indecisive and naïve. No. It applied to that horrid feeling when I realised that some new game was about to be played, and, in spite of all my careful preparations according to the objective seduction plan, no standard technique was of any use.

"Derek still at the library?"

"Mmm."

I sauntered over to the table, pulled out a chair and sat down. This manoeuvre seemed to take up the space of about an hour and a half.

"It's funny," said Julie, putting her head on one side and twisting her Biro to and fro in her hands, "you've settled in quite easily haven't you?"

"I suppose I have."

71

"After all that . . . fuss between us."

"Yes."

Another one of the pauses. Not as bad this time.

"I suppose," I said, "I was incredibly naïve then."

Pause again. This time much, much worse.

"Oh we both were," said Julie, "we both were."

I put out one hand flat on the table. It was now about six inches from Julie's arm. Why was it, I thought to myself, that when I'd had her *breast* out I'd felt absolutely nothing, and that now I felt something, whatever it was, extremely violently? Why was it that now that I'd written off the idea of loving her, written off the idea of love itself, I felt so incredibly randy? I tapped the table. Oh God. A slight movement from her.

"It's really stupid, Julie, but—"

"But what?"

"I think I might kiss you or something."

We looked sideways at each other. The room had suddenly acquired the characteristics of an echo chamber. The remark hung in the air, bouncing back from the walls. She allowed her hand (or was it just an accident?) to come closer to mine and I allowed my hand (too late now anyway) to touch hers and she didn't draw back and I moved round the table, awkward, in a hell of a hurry, stooped across and kissed her all in one movement. Thinking "What if the pauses have all been in my head? What if the looks have all been a mistake? What if—?" But suddenly my mouth was on hers and her lips were parting, like soft paper, to the touch and my tongue had found hers and we were kissing in a way we never had but should have done in that room of hers in Bardwell Road, mouths glued together . . . is this how Derek kisses, I thought, is this how they were kissing that time when I . . . ?

"Yes," she was saying, "yes. Go on. Go on."

And my hands were fumbling with her dress. And she wasn't stiffening or moving away from me but guiding my hands and here right here in the kitchen I was helping her to take off her dress and JESUS CHRIST her knickers, her real-live knickers and she was unhooking her bra BLOODY HELL this was all happening fast it

72

was happening very fast and it occurred to me that I had better take off my trousers (why does it take so bloody long to *damn* caught in the shoes no right shoe first very unerotic but it has to be done and) JESUS CHRIST she's TAKEN OFF HER KNICKERS AND I CAN SEE ALL OF IT OH GOD OH GOD OH GOD the socks now never mind the damn socks right up to her pressing the body against hers she decided to do this ages ago she was always prepared to fuck me but the only thing that put her off was thinking I wasn't groovy enough and of course she needed the security after Harris (what a name!) and it really suited her when I was Good Friends after the wedding and those looks she's been giving me all along are the looks of a conspirator and CHRIST I AM TOUCHING HER NAKED BEHIND I REALLY AM. I REALLY AM. THIS IS AMAZING.

However (I thought). Just for the moment. Concentrate on getting her on the floor. On the rush matting. Not worrying about the curtains. Make it all smooth. Very easy to mess it up.

Ask yourself:

1. Will it go up?
2. Will it stay up?
3. Is it big enough?

However (I thought). We are into Insertion Module Phase One. And, aided by her, this seems to be passing off satisfactorily. We have insertion, yes, we have insertion, we have the penis fully inserted and loaded. Now. Move the bum up and down. *That's* right. *Not* too fast. A one and a two and a three and a four. And, while moving the bum up and down, we suggest you embrace your partner. I *know* it's difficult. Who said it would be easy? Elbows. Elbows.

Oh God (I thought) oh Jesus God this is nice this is incredibly nice.

SHE WAS MAKING NOISES. Just like in the books or as overheard with Derek. Very satisfactory. The faraway moan, as of the wind in trees at the bottom of our garden the one we had in Mill Hill with a tennis court at the end where Mr Jessup used to play *whacking* the ball and *whacking* the ball and it's rather like climbing a hill only the higher up the hill the flatter it becomes

73

it's more like treading a hill, treading the earth down and getting

TEN-NINE-EIGHT-SEVEN-FOUR-THREE-TWO-ONE...

AAAAAAAAARCHIOUMNNNNNN!!!!!!!!!!

And shake and shake. And—

(Is she all right?) I thought.

She was fine. And both of us heard the door behind open. Softly. And knew, without looking—me by the prickles all down my back and Julie because she was, must have been, looking straight at him, that Derek stood in the doorway a full second before he closed it again, softly, and went off down the hall and out into the street, closing the door behind him. And Julie didn't say anything at first, being, I supposed afterwards, too horrified or too polite, and I, of course, was equally reticent, but, as usual, being unable to stop thinking, thought:

I wanted her. I wanted her a long time ago. And she didn't want me. I hadn't grown up enough. My face didn't fit. Being grown up means putting on faces and screwing other people's wives and lying until you're blue-faced and never really being with the people you trust and love. She'd grown up, somehow, when I first met her. And now I've had her, got what I wanted, and I suppose I'm grown up. But why did I feel sick and lonely? Why did I have more certainty when I was walking her back to her room all those months ago? And why, why, why do they only give you what you want when you don't need it any more?

Usual stuff, I thought to myself, as I climbed off her. Neither of us had said anything about Derek. Yet. Usual stuff, I thought again, groping for my clothes. Some gremlin appeared to have got hold of them while we were at it and scattered them about the room. Usual stuff—choking on the food of the Gods.

"Did—"

"Yes?"

"I mean," she said tentatively, "it's weird. But I thought that maybe the door..."

"I didn't notice anything," I said.

"No," said Julie, "some fantasy of mine."

Still naked. Oh bloody hell. And the space between us now, like that man had said in the poem, was about a couple of years.

74

When I'd dressed, I said I had to go into town. We didn't talk much before I went, except, after one of the new variety of pauses—the cold-and-impossible-to-bridge ones—Julie said, her back to me, looking out of the window:

"He knew what was going on."

"Yes."

"But he didn't try to stop it."

"No."

"He doesn't know how."

She turned back to me as she said this, and gave me a look I thought I recognised. I'd seen it once before, and it didn't take long to remember where. It was that day she'd come to see me in the Warneford. It was a little-girl-lost look, but there was a wealth of cleverness to it. And it was then I realised that all the time I'd been seducing her, it was her who had, as they say, been calling the shots. One step ahead all the time, cool as you like. Picking up both of us when she needed us. I didn't say anything else though. In that one look, the whole situation between us was understood. If we wanted to do it again that would be fine. Derek wouldn't interfere. He didn't know how. But we would have to be mature and discreet and arrange times and places, and I would never be more than a distraction for her. Which was perhaps why, although I'd failed to seduce her first time round, and had, now, apparently succeeded, I still felt locked out, cheated. And, even worse than that, I began to suspect that as much of the fault lay in me, neither rôle—Jilted Lover or Clever Seducer—was me. All I'd enjoyed at any stage of the game was the few moments, when, forgetting the purpose in hand, I'd been able to be myself.

"Do you know—" I said.

"What?"

"That time you and me and Derek went to Banbury in the car..."

"Mmm."

"It was really nice."

"Yes."

A pause.

"And when we were in Sussex that time."

"That was *before*."

"Before you got married."

"So it was."

"When I was going out with you, remember?"

"I enjoyed all that," said Julie, "honestly I did."

"Yes," I said, "me too. Me too."

She turned round towards me then and came back to the table. We both sat. Outside someone was trying to start a car.

"The thing about me and you," said Julie, "is that we're very, very dishonest people. We neither of us are prepared to trust each other. And we have to have someone as a scapegoat or a longstop or something. If you think about it that's what we've been doing. I mean when we were going out you were always trying to get me to join in in some romantic spree or other, to commit myself completely. But I know and you know that I couldn't trust you. And now, with Derek, we both know that we could give each other a lot of . . . pleasure and *both* of us could use Derek to pick up the pieces. Right? Because in spite of all those jokes you made about him I mean the thing about him is he's . . ."

"He's a really nice guy," I said, "that's the thing about him."

"Exactly. And we're not, are we? We're not really nice guys. We spend most of our lives in some transport of superiority over other people, you with a whole string of private jokes that I can see going on in your head because you're incredibly transparent, Martin, and me I suppose by thinking I can arrange the world to suit my convenience. Which up to a point I can. But it's no good is it? I mean—we only seem to make the other lonely."

"Is that how you felt?"

"When?"

"Just now."

"That's how I felt. I mean Jesus don't you ever stop thinking and looking at yourself and running little commentaries in your head? When you're making *love* for God's sake and—"

"I know, Julie, but you see—"

"What?"

"Maybe I need help or something."

76

"Maybe we both do," said Julie, "but not from each other."

She got up then and I did too. We didn't need to say that I would be packing up my things soon and moving out. We didn't say good-bye. Both of us, I think, thought that we would meet again after I'd left, even if it wasn't as lovers. How could two people so similar not meet again? Everything she had said was true and most of it I had thought already. That didn't make her saying it any easier. As I turned into the Main Road at Summertown, I saw Derek sitting by himself in the window of a café. There was a cup of coffee in front of him but he wasn't interested in it. He was interested in the table and the way his fingers were drumming on it, tapping out the seconds. Waiting to go home. Waiting for his best friend to finish screwing his wife.

I've finished, I thought, as I ran towards a bus. I've finished that for good and all.

There. That was how it happened. All I have to do is to get back to that pile of papers in the corner and work it up into a fictional narrative. Getting the boot into Julie good and proper. I might grant them a groatsworth of tragedy at the end, the slight hint that my hero is not always able to combine the best features of the Mekon and Johnny Weissmuller. But then people like their heroes to have weaknesses, it makes them more lovable.

Oh it needs work. A lot of work. And writing this journal helps me to see things that are wrong ... but it will be finished soon. And then (oh joy and oh rapture) ... the Dedication!!!!!!!

> To Julie
> Hoping she likes it ...

Not bad. Or perhaps:

> To Julie
> In memory of the time we spent together

Heh heh heh.

Which reminds me. While racing ahead with my journal I have not only been ignoring the novel, I have allowed my lunch to get completely cold. There is no sound of door opening and closing or of footsteps in the hall. Have Oswald and Ellen gone out to

77

lunch? I wouldn't put it past them. I resist the temptation to gorge myself on things like the design of the dust-jacket (possibly a picture of Me at Oxford?) and address myself to my wife and lodger.

Now that work for the day is over, I think I might allow myself to open the letter. I feel just about strong enough for one of Ellen's jokes. I notice how thick it is. Probably a bundle of blank sheets of paper, with a tiny coded message, hidden at the bottom of one of the sheets. Here goes.

Not good. It reads:

Dear Martin,

HAVE YOU HAD YOUR LUNCH?

We thought not. We can usually calculate your every movement. Often we peer in at you through the keyhole. Oh yes.

IT'S NICE. GO ON. EAT IT UP!!

This is to say that Oswald and I are running away together. We are *not* having an affair even if your oh-so-obvious-mind immediately jumps to that conclusion. We are both fed up with SEX. There is quite enough of it these days and Oswald's Thing has fallen off due to the over-use of RADOX (a bath salt).

THERE'S MUSTARD IF YOU WANT IT AS WELL!!!

Actually we are fed up with

A.   Cleaning the house.
B.   Doing the launderette.
C.   Getting money for you from Harrods.

While you sit up there writing a load of old crap about something or other. We are young, Martin! We have our lives before us! There are things to do, films to see, people to meet!

IF YOU DON'T WANT MUSTARD THERE'S KETCHUP. YOU LIKE KETCHUP DON'T YOU? EH?

As for the mortgage, about which you are so humorous. We suggest you either pay it or sell the house and move. Somewhere like Ullapool or Stornaway, far away from publishers. They seem to have a bad effect on you, as, indeed, do theatre managements, agents, reviewers, etc.

ON THE REMAINING PAGES ARE SOME IDEAS FOR PASSING THE TIME AFTER OUR DEPARTURE.

Bye bye Martin. You probably won't even notice we've gone.

> Regards,
> Oswald and Ellen—"The Dynamic Duo"
> (available for Weddings and Bar-mitzvahs)

P.S.   Our address is:

ROOM 5005,
THE HOLIDAY INN,
YAOUNDE,
WEST CAMEROON,
AFRICA.

One of their jokes. Or rather—one of Ellen's jokes. The handwriting is all hers. Another one of their jokes. Then why aren't I laughing? The rest of the pages are blank but for short suggestions like—"Walking", "Window Shopping", "Picking your nose" and so on. And, on the last page, it says:

"I BET YOU GO TO THE WINDOW TO SEE IF OSWALD'S CAR *REALLY* HAS GONE."

Funny. I was going to do that. Funny. But I'm still not laughing.

PART TWO

10

> Pity at the roundabout
> Is weeping, as the trucks head north
> For another December . . .

I've tried just about everything since she left, and, like many others before me, ended up with poetry. Not bad poetry or good poetry, just poetry, written to try and make me feel better. And no question of sending it anywhere, or ever, really, trying anything in that line again. It's done enough damage. I can remember Rimbaud's line, when he'd jacked it all in and was running guns in Abyssinia or somewhere. Someone had asked him what he thought about literature—"Oh that shit," he said, "I used to have something to do with those people . . ." And then went on to say what a shower they were.

And they are a shower. Why I even wanted to join them I can't imagine. Racked by mutual jealousy, screwing each other's wives. I have to ask myself. Did I really want Ellen to be a Writer's Wife, one of those middle-aged women who look like Brazil nuts and can only talk about residuals, and what they did to "our" play in Tanganyika. No. This is the voice of a Rimbaud. A Rimbaud who renounced a non-existent career (no less of a sacrifice). I'm not actually going to tear *up* the novel. I added some more to it last week and there's nearly fifty thousand words there.

Do I believe this? Obviously not. I could as soon think of jacking in writing as of flying to the moon. I have, after all, invested some thousands of man hours in the activity—in dining-rooms-after-everyone's-gone-to-bed, in offices-when-I-thought-no-one-was-watching-me or (luxurious!) studies, rooms-of-my-own like this, with the cracked window and the doorstopper—four square yards of beautiful, beautiful solitude. I'm temporarily demoralised, as I was the other week, that's all. But I have faith in the thing, in the same way as I have faith that I shall be alive tomorrow. It may be an unwarrantable assumption, but life would be unbearable without it.

Let's go back over progress. The new thirty thousand words came, first in a rush, just after she'd gone, then two trickles. I did eight hundred and twenty words yesterday. I spent more time counting the bastards than writing them. I'm clearer now, about my narrator. After Roger Beamish, the Derek character, barges in, he breaks off the narration, and there's a long dialogue section, in which we discover, that our narrator, too, has been hurt by a woman. And I've called him Stephen Judge. Geddit? The other radical change is that I haven't called it Oxford. It was a terrible hack location. I've called it The College. After all—there are tens of thousands of people in full-time higher education. There are *areas* of their experience that must be shared. Universality again. And it's those elements, not the texture of Gothic stone walls or the sigh of the wind over the bleeding Cherwell, that I want to get. It's the Pinter trick. Write a melodrama, cut off its arms and legs and you have something infinitely sinister, infinitely suggestive ... The other problem is drunk scenes—I seem to have about eight drunk scenes (which may well reflect my own preoccupations but might bore the non-drinking audience). Anything else? Well ... maybe too much description of foreign parts, especially Switzerland, a country I've only been to once about ten years ago. Otherwise fine. Just talking about the thing makes me feel better. I will get back to it.

Two women in my life, just the two, officer. One dark, one red-head, and both haunting me. One left a long time ago, and the other was ripped out of the womb of this house a short time ago, but they're both here, over my shoulder, grinning, mocking, chattering "We told you so. We told you so. We told you so." I go into the front room (sanded floors, unread paperbacks in neat lines across the walls) and I sit by the stereo. Half past seven comes and I realise—I AM WAITING FOR MY DINNER. Gawd. By eight o'clock I readjust. Ellen isn't going to come through the door laden with parcels, clicking through to the hall like a Gestapo officer. Ellen isn't going to say "Are you going to the off-licence?" And I, in my turn, am not going to reply—"Darling, can *you*?" Ellen has gone. Departed Ellen. Leftover life to kill and all that jazz.

Sometimes, when I wake in the morning, I could swear that I see her. I swear I hear her, licking her lips at the other end of the bed, and feel the swish of air as her behind swings out and up under the bedclothes. I see her in crowds, of course, all the time, brows knitted, shoulders hunched, storming along like a cross girl in a children's comic. I remember once, her mother and I were sitting in the front room, looking out at the street, when this grim Wagnerian figure strode past, hair out behind her, glaring fiercely at the pavement. It was Ellen. She didn't stop but strode on, as if late for an appointment with the Angel of Death. "My God," I thought, "what has happened? Brainstorm? Sudden urge to travel?" It was none of these things. She'd just overshot the house. She reappeared some minutes later, grinning feebly and doing her Caveman Shot Through The Knees impression.

People don't just disappear. The ripples of their personality, the shock waves of someone else's ego, can take years to subside. Some rooms in the house I can't bear to go into. For the first two days, the lavatory was quite a tricky one. A common household event was for me to hurl open the door only to see Ellen sitting on the pedestal, a picture of maidenly modesty.

"Oh," she'd say, "I'm sorry. I'm so sorry."

"Fine," I'd say, "fine."

And we'd smile, shyly, encouragingly at each other. And I would close the door.

I have been forced into using the facilities offered by Oswald's bathroom upstairs, a nightmare tundra of old Gold Leaf packets, copies of the *Daily Mail* and editions of various abstruse economic journals. Oswald's only attempt at décor has been to sellotape a picture of Hitler and Doenitz above the bath and to write on the wall underneath, in Biro, "The Editor of the Birmingham

85

Evening Gazette shares a joke with a Senior Colleague". The awful thing is that, as well as missing Ellen, I miss Oswald terribly. I miss the sound of his coming in at four in the morning, the cheerful rattle of his ignition keys and the muttered oath as he crashes into something in the hall. I miss the rhythms of his life, the buying and emptying of bottles of Scotch and the late-night phone calls to the *Daily Mail* to the sub-editors, hungry for Communist conspiracies. I miss them both. I admit it.

First of all—why did she go? Didn't I do it enough? Did I spend too much time writing? Was it because I wasn't famous? I can't do anything about the third problem but the first two can be easily avoided. The way I look at it is this—if I'm going to spend time writing I *have* to be famous. If I'm not famous that means I don't have to spend time writing, which leaves me time to screw. By accepting my third limitation I solve the first two. Good resolution number one.

Oh Jesus though. It's no good. I get so lonely. Get up at twelve, mooch around, phone old friends who aren't in, or who...

The real problem is none of my faults seems quite enough to make her walk out on me. There must be some concrete reason. If Oswald wasn't such an old friend I think I'd start suspecting him. The other day, in fact, I did go up to his room to uncover evidence—a love-letter or, possibly, an article of her clothing. I found nothing. The only alien object in the place was a pair of my underpants and an *A to Z* I thought I'd lost about a year ago.

She's only been gone, perhaps I should point out, four days. But it feels a lot longer. And by the end of the week—damn. Someone at the door.

A letter. I can't stand this. I don't want to open it. Maybe I won't read it. An *airmail* letter by God.

Dear Martin,
       I suppose you know by now that it's all over between us. I love Oswald and Oswald loves me. Don't try and find us for we are too far away...

Could that be it? Or will it be a real *Who's Afraid of Virginia*

Woolf touch—ten gin-stained pages of below-the-belt stabs.

Open it, Steel. Open it. Be a man.

I remember the day I first met Ellen—in an office in Bush House, of all places. I was working for the African Service of the BBC and I was sitting, my ear glued to a portable tape-recorder, when this girl walked in —medium height, red-haired and a rather amused expression. Opposite me was a youth called Carter, with whom I was working at the time. Lucky old Carter, I thought—as well as the red hair and the amused expression, she had large, resilient looking breasts and eyes that spoke of pleasant mutual siestas. She strode across to one of the desks and sat down. Playing it really cool. She didn't even look at Carter and neither did he, by word or gesture, indicate that he knew her. I've never seen two people play it so cool. After a while a very large black man stuck his head round the door (an event not unusual in the African Service of the BBC). He said:

"Hi, Martin!"

"Hi!" I said.

"Who was the spade?" said Carter to me, when the black man had gone.

"The Prime Minister of Botswana," said the girl. And she got up and walked out.

"What's got into her?" said Carter to me.

"Don't ask me," I said to Carter, "she's your girlfriend."

"She bloody well isn't," said Carter. "I thought she was *your* girlfriend."

"Afraid not," I said.

We both looked at each other. Then, as one man, we got up, walked to the corridor, and peered out. The girl with red hair was glued up against the wall, about six inches from my nose. When I stuck my head round the door, she said, slowly and patiently, as if to a young child:

> Life is a cycle of endless song,
> A medley of extemporania.
> Love is a thing that can never go wrong,
> And I am Marie of Roumania.

"Dorothy Parker," I said.

"No," said the girl with red hair, "Ellen Jackson."

"Hi Ellen," said Carter, pushing past me, "I *thought* I recognised you."

"Oh," said the girl, "how nice. *But*, Mr Sandwickers, if you use the word 'spade' again in my presence I shall report you to the Race Relations Board. A spade is a garden implement. O.K?" There was a touch of sharpness in the way she said this. She then turned on her heel and walked off down the corridor, wiggling her behind at us satirically, in the manner of a secretary in a British film of the Fifties. I turned to Carter and said:

"What was with the Sandwickers bit?"

"Search me," said Carter, "but what a bum."

We watched the bum until it was out of sight, went back into the office and had a long heart-to-heart about whether Carter was a racialist or not. Ellen's like that. She has high standards, and tends to get fellows examining their darker and nastier selves. The joke was that I found out later that she rather fancied Carter and had come into the office with the express purpose of picking him up. If I hadn't come across with the right name for the quotation, I might never have stood a chance.

I won't open the letter yet. Not just yet.

I suppose I could always put it with the stuff from Julie and the letters from the publishers and really expand the novel—seven-hundred-pages touch, a real Odyssey of the spirit. Slowly though, Steel. I think you should lay off the novel for a bit. Are you ready for it? I'm not. And, I have to admit it, that depresses me. It's O.K. to be an aesthete but I should be a more resilient aesthete. It's no good—I can't be a real artist. When something like this happens to me I can't work. I can't bear the idea of work whereas Proust or Joyce would have been knocking out the thousand words a day even if their wives were being screwed in the next room. But I'm not Proust or Joyce and I'm thoroughly demoralised about the novel. In my weaker moments I seriously consider using it as a draught excluder. Oh, parts of it are fine, but—SHUT UP! DEFEATISM!

I notice with interest that, although it's an airmail letter, the postmark says SWISS COTTAGE 4.30 p.m. Wednesday. It's no good. I might as well open it.

Dear Martin,

      By the time you read this, Oswald and I will be a long way away. Barnet to be precise. Do not try to find us. Barnet is a big place and your little feet are very flat!

      KISS KISS KISS XXXXXX

      How is the *house*? Are you getting your dinner O.K.? How's the NOVEL?

      Oswald is writing a novel. It is called PIG-TIME and it is about two pigs who learn how to dance. It is a novel for children. Barnet is very strange and Oswald does not always understand the dialect, but I have booked us into a little "bodega".

      IF YOU REQUIRE FURTHER INFORMATION I SUGGEST YOU GO TO THE TUDOR CLOSE PUBLIC HOUSE, RICHMOND, WHERE A CONTACT OF OURS WILL MEET YOU. TIME 7 P.M. NEXT FRIDAY.

      I hope you are not "wanking" while I'm away.

      Your Wifikins

P.S.   Oswald says hullo and would like to put his mark!

Beneath this—a large stain, made, I suspect, by brown ale, and a scrawling, disorganised script I recognise as Oswald's. It says: "Hi Mart! Problems this end!!"

I put the letter down. Maybe she has flipped. Maybe her mind has finally gone. It's a possibility. A too great concern for practical jokes can lead one to insanity I suppose. Maybe this is all a ploy to persuade me to have children. My flesh creeps at the idea.

From time to time I can see both of them—Julie and Ellen. They are walking hand in hand. They stop at the top of the road, turn and smile. And, in a coffee bar opposite, Oswald and Derek are talking. Oswald is acting the way he does when he's with me, gesturing to emphasise a point, and Derek is nodding slowly, dumb-wisely. What are they all really but a pack of sods? And

what way to revenge myself on them but by writing? Eh?
No, no. That way madness lies. Or does it?
The Tudor Close. Friday. Tonight.

I I

Midnight Friday

Funny thing. I started this journal intending to get a novel about
Julie out of it. But I'm coming to the conclusion that if I don't get
a novel about Ellen out of it, then I'm shirking my
responsibilities. Despite the depressed mood earlier today, seeing
Oswald this evening has really set me going. The blood races,
partly, I must conclude, because of alcohol. And I get the feeling
that this novel (the Julie and Ellen double-decker) is going to be a
hell of a lot better than the last one.

You see, the real problem with all that Julie material was quite
simply that I hadn't worked it through. I still hated her, or rather
didn't hate her but I hadn't in any sense resolved my attitude
towards her, and so I couldn't piece a story together from the
remembered fragments of our life. There was a moment of
affection here, a pure piece of vitriol there, and, all the time, I was
writing about someone else—Stephen Jarrett or whatever you
like to call him, not me, but a dead version of myself under glass.
The Ellen thing has woken a whole crowd of impressions, dreams
and responses; I feel that, in some mysterious way, I am coming
to understand myself and that, by understanding myself I could
really get to write a decent book. Not a revenge book or a love
book or a *roman à clef*—just a book.

Bit pissed. I haven't even bothered to draw the curtains and I
can look across to the houses opposite and the night sky, lighter
than the roofs. A hot night again. Only a moment of wavering,
Steel, earlier this afternoon—now you know what you have to do.

91

First of all—get down everything that happened with Oswald this evening, because the double-decker novel is going to include Oswald as well. By his equivocal behaviour, he has earned himself a place in fiction.

I got to the Tudor Close early. It's a large, coachhouse-style pub, overlooking the river. Inside—a well-lighted room, marred by several youths in T-shirts and huge stomachs, discussing the specific gravity of obscure varieties of Real Ale. I got myself a pint and heard Oswald's voice behind me:

"Hi Mart!"

"Oh. Hi!"

I turned. He was jigging from one foot to the other with suppressed nervous energy and grinning. Widening his eyes, he said:

"You're early!"

"Yes," I said.

He was still jigging as we sat down, and, another thing Oswald does when nervous—pushing his lower lip forward and trying to touch the tip of his nose with his tongue. I let him get an inch down his glass and said:

"How is she?"

Once again, Oswald seemed on the verge of laughter.

"Oh she's fine. Fine," he said. He had now added to the pushing forward of the lower lip another one of the gestures from stock. This consists of scratching his head violently and then shaking it, as if suddenly blinded by dandruff. I decided to leave the talking to him. After a while he said:

"Thing *is*, Mart—"

And then stopped. There was plenty going on in the pause though. He did another scratch and jabbed violently at the table with his forefinger for about thirty seconds.

"Thing *is*—"

"Where is she?" I asked quickly and concisely.

"She's . . . er . . . in the Barnet area," said Oswald, looking up. He spoke the last three words in the tones of a hardened newsman imparting a valuable secret.

"Whereabouts in the Barnet area?"

"Ah," said Oswald, transfixed with embarrassment, "ah. You see—she said I wasn't to tell you that."

"For *Christ's* sake!"

"It's bad, Mart, I know. I mean really bad."

"I'll say it is, Ossie."

Oswald went off into another round of pantomime agitation. When he'd finished, he said:

"Look—"

"Look what?"

"I don't know what's going on. Honest. Any more than you do."

"But Ossie. I mean—has she flipped or what?"

"No no no. She hasn't flipped. She's very, very together actually."

"Ah."

A pause.

"Well *I'm* not together, Ossie."

"No. No."

Another pause.

"Look I'm really sorry about this, Mart."

"Well don't be. I mean it isn't your fault."

I recalled similar evenings in pubs in the Shepherd's Bush area, when Oswald and I had discussed his many girlfriends. What did Judy mean when she said that? Will Suzy be upset when she hears about Jane and Fran? And so on. And, in the past, I've always played Uncle in these confrontations. The rôle of Uncle sits uneasily on Oswald.

"She'll be in touch anyway," said Oswald.

"*When?*"

"I don't know really. I mean that's up to her."

"*Jesus!*"

"The only thing she asked me to say, Mart, was this. That she's sorry but she needs a little time to think something out. I mean I don't know *what* she wants to think out but she said she just needs time."

There was a lot more humming and hawing and scratching and jabbing but that was about all I got out of him. We moved,

93

imperceptibly, from discussing Ellen to discussing the Communist Party, and from the Communist Party, by some subtle conversational sleight of hand that only Oswald could manage, to Real Ale. At half past nine, he said:

"Look—"

"Yes?"

"Gotta go. Sorry."

"Fine," I said.

"She'll be in touch. Honest."

He looked at me conspiratorially from under his tangled mass of hair. Something still seemed to be amusing him, and, he seemed to be saying, when I knew it, it might amuse me too. He tugged his forelock violently and got up from the table. Then we said good-bye again. I stood where I was and Oswald went out through the saloon-bar door. At the door he turned, thrust his jaw out as far as it would go (quite a long way) and gave me the thumbs-up sign. Then he was gone.

You see—the thought occurs to me that, in many ways, my relationship with Ellen is exactly paralleled by my relationship with Julie. In both affairs there was another guy involved, although in very different capacities. Oswald may well be having it off with her, even though I find that difficult to believe when I'm with him. And, in both cases the affair ended with me liking the male go-between as much, if not more, than the lady concerned. Or is that true of Ellen? I don't dislike her simply because she's left me. I get violent feelings towards her but I hold on to what we had. But what did we have? Oh shit.

All that might add up to something, mightn't it?

"Stephen Jarrett, a repressed homosexual, is involved in yet another meaningless relationship. To support his sexual confidence, he brings in his friend, *Oswald*, a young bisexual journalist...." Maybe not. The idea of Oswald as bisexual is frankly laughable. If he was in bed with another man, he'd probably start discussing Real Ale or the Communist Party. Although I suppose that homosexuals occasionally discuss such matters.

Get a grip, Steel. I haven't finished with Ellen the way I have

94

with Julie. If I wasn't distant enough from the Julie material, I haven't a hope in hell of making sense out of my relationship with Ellen—yet. And, if I needed time and consideration to get the Stephen character off the ground, how much more time do I need to work out a novel involving the Stephen character, a Julie figure, *and* a stand-in for Ellen? This journal, as always, will be a place for working out my feelings. When I've worked them out, I'll start on the book. I don't know whether the book will be hostile or friendly—as usual I'll only be able to discover the truth of my feelings by writing them down. Now. Ellen and I are mature adults having a mature problem. She may even be in trouble, in need of my help. This possibility cannot be ruled out.

"Martin—"

"Yes, darling—"

"Martin, I just had to get away because—"

"Because why, darling?"

"Because..."

Well, because what?

The other problem with this is, when she's not here I find it very difficult to remember her and precisely how she would behave in any given situation. It's the thing I was talking through earlier. Ellen as Fictional Woman just doesn't seem real to me at all, probably because I don't understand her. Or don't want to understand her. One of the essential features of a fictional character is that you (the author) have the power to determine exactly what they will do next, and one of the most important features of the Ellen/Me set-up is that I never have the faintest idea what's in store. I didn't really, from the day we met. I recall, unwillingly, the day we decided to get married. Early spring in Hyde Park—the two of us lying about six feet away from each other.

"Well," I said, "I don't know. We might as well—"

"What?"

"You know. I mean we might as *well* get—"

"Get what?"

"Get ... You know."

"Oh *that*."

95

She turned over on her stomach and looked at me, amused as usual. She rested her chin on her hands. I screwed my neck round painfully.

"Do you think?" I said.

"Fine," she said, and then she got to her feet. She crossed over to me and prodded me in the stomach with her toe. The sun was behind her and she looked very pretty. "But," she went on, "you said it first, little man. You said it first. Okey dokey?"

"Sure I said it first," I replied, "what's wrong with that?"

And then we looked at each other for quite a long time, like heavyweight wrestlers sizing each other up. And then I bought her a ring. And she said DIAMONDS MAKE IT PERFECT ESPECIALLY FROM BRAVINGTONS.

It is a wrestling match, me and Ellen. And she is simply making a particularly clever move. I have to keep very cool and very clever and very mature and get this whole thing together.

And I can best start that by carrying out my plan. Thoughts on paper. And start by getting down the rest of what happened this evening. In order to do that I'll need coffee. Balzac nearly poisoned himself with the stuff, why not me? A lot of coffee. Oh my head my head my head.

12

8 a.m. Saturday

I didn't get time to finish the course last night. After I went down into the kitchen and made myself a cup of coffee I felt so bloody depressed I wasn't fit for anything. One of those "everything is useless" moods again. It's always worse just before you go to bed. And, looking back at what I've written since she's gone, what depresses me unutterably about it is its total lack of clarity or consistency. One minute I'm saying she's a bitch, next minute I've got us down as two wonderful adversaries à la Beatrice and Benedick and next minute (i.e. now) I'm sitting on the ground and howling because I'm twenty-seven years old and I haven't got a clue about anything. The only things I seem to understand about myself are the mistakes I made eight years ago.

To get back to me and Oswald in the Tudor Close, Richmond. Or rather, me without Oswald in the Tudor Close. After he'd gone, I went to the outer door and stood outside. It was a warm night, and people were spread out on the grass above the pub, glasses all round them. Oswald didn't see me. He walked to his car, patting his pockets in a desperate search for his ignition key. Half-way there he panicked and wheeled round towards the pub again, head lowered, but, after a few paces—miracle!—he found it. Then back to the car. He went round to the driver's door, which doesn't open except from the inside. Tried that. No good. Then back to the opposite door.

While he was playing with the lock and generally behaving like a burglar, I went across to my car, started up and, when he pulled out of the car-park, I followed him. We went along by the

97

river, through Richmond town centre, and then up the main road towards Hammersmith. At Hammersmith we turned up to Shepherd's Bush, then up Wood Lane towards Kilburn. It's not difficult tailing Oswald, as he's not aware of any other cars on the road, let alone a car that is behind him. From time to time I could see him scratching his head in silhouette. The only danger was when, as he sometimes does, he decided to "make up time". This manoeuvre involves driving straight at the rear lights of the car in front and braking sharply at the last moment. He did this all the way along the North Circular road, but, by the time we had got to Hendon, he had relaxed. By this time I was getting fairly nervous. It seemed reasonable to suppose that he was going to Ellen's.

In the end, we stopped by a row of shops, somewhere between Finchley and Whetstone on the main road north to Barnet. I stayed in the car. Oswald got out and I saw him rummaging in the back seat. He emerged with a large sack, which he flung across his shoulder, Father Christmas style, and, with a wild look up and down the road, walked off *direction* Barnet. By this time I was convinced that he was engaged in something suspicious. Headlines flashed through my mind—"JOURNALIST STEALS CLOTHING FOR FRIEND'S WIFE'S LOVER! TEN YEARS." Oswald certainly looked even more furtive than usual—were that possible. I got out of the car, and, as I watched, he reached his destination.

I must have been drunk. He was, of course, going to the launderette. A large sign over the door said "THE COIN LAUNDRY".

It was possible that he'd come all this way simply with the intention of sampling this particular branch. I crossed over to the other side of the road, where I have a good view of the launderette's wildly over-lit interior, from my position in the shadows. Oswald was heaping trousers and shirts and (yes dresses oh surely not Ellen's?) into a machine, watched admiringly by two old ladies, dressed as if for church. He seemed quite absorbed. I crossed over the road. When he had finished, Oswald pressed his face to the porthole and peered up to see if there was any more room. One of the old ladies tapped him on the shoulder, and Oswald turned, in the manner of Dracula startled by an unscheduled sunrise. The old lady pointed towards something on the floor. Oswald gaped. The other lady bent down, with great difficulty, and held it out at arm's length, like an angler with a prizewinning fish. From my position, I could see it quite clearly—a black brassière, with lace at the front. It was an item of clothing I had removed several hundred times, in moments of passion—although, to speak the truth, more often than not, it had been removed for me of recent years. Ellen's. Shi–i–it. I had at least twenty minutes, so I went into a pub down the road.

Had I been following someone less predictable, I might well have made more mistakes. But I was very clever. I knew Oswald would make straight for the pub as soon as the machine started to operate, but I knew also that he would make for the saloon bar. As this particular pub was one of the few left in North London which still tried to siphon off the working classes in case their carpets got dirty, I went into the public.

The pub was laid out in an extraordinary fashion. The bar divided the two halves of the place, and, although the barman moved freely between the two, in order to avoid the risk of saloon-bar customers catching a glimpse of a proletarian face, the management had erected a kind of screen. This meant that, although you couldn't see the faces or bodies of your drinking companions across the way, you could see their drinks (at least when they were up at the bar) and their arms—up to about six inches before the elbow. The effect was rather that of a surreal puppet show.

After about five minutes, when I was safely ensconced on a stool intended, I had no doubt, for some senile local, I looked through to the saloon bar, and caught a glimpse of a pair of hands transferring coins between each other at a great speed. As I watched, the right hand went up in a nervous little bid for attention. Somebody brought the hand a pint glass of chemically foaming ale. The pint glass disappeared, then came back into vision, seriously depleted. The hands were joined by the elbows. Then, both hands and elbows started to do a lot of gesture work, implying that their owner was in deep and intimate conversation with the barman. After a very short space of time, the pint glass was empty, and the hands held it up for a re-fill. Oswald. Had to be.

I ordered another drink and wondered whether Oswald was actually living with Ellen. He was washing her clothes that was for sure, but (a new and frightening angle this) he could just be covering up for another man. I still think this is possible, actually. It wouldn't be untypical for Oswald to feel something absurd like "I owe a duty to them both" and "I ought to respect both their wishes." You can't do that, of course, in an affair of this sort. Even neutrality forces you into some kind of alliance. If things go on long enough and Oswald carries on washing clothes for this guy who's knocking off Ellen I shall doubtless end up hating him. After all, it's one thing to pretend to be neutral and it's quite another to hare all the way up to Barnet to make sure that your best friend's wife's lover has an adequate supply of clean—

Grip, Steel. Stop it now. Stop it. Slowly. Slo—o—owly. To get back to last night.

Anyway. After the hands had conveyed the contents of three pint glasses to the out-of-vision mouth, something horrible happened. Just to their right—a yellow blouse, two bare forearms and two slim but practical hands, covered in rings, arrived. They touched one of Oswald's arms, lightly, affectionately, and then drummed on the bar. Oswald's arms, in the fullness of time, brought them a tomato juice. Ellen. I don't think I've ever looked at her hands that closely before. I thought how much of her character they revealed and how ... Not good. Not good. I can still see the conversation between the two pairs of hands, delicate, intriguing, curiously sexy and provoking me to old suspicions about the nature of their owners and the relationship between them. And Ellen's ... an adulterer's hands? A hangman's hands? Do they look any different? And, the thought occurs to me, will they look any different next Wednesday?

I'm jumping ahead of the story. Remember the position you have assigned yourself, Steel. You are a calm, interested, but responsible observer. You are prepared to learn. You must not jump to conclusions about people or things. You will proceed with the events of last night. Dalek-like, I tell myself to keep cool.

When they left, I waited a safe number of minutes and, of course, followed them back to the launderette. But I didn't have the guts to follow them inside. I don't know what it was. Seeing him and her, laughing, getting on—I was reminded of that fundamental and awful truth, that, when you're not there, people get on fine without you. They carry on nodding and smiling and disagreeing with each other just the way they will after you're dead. And, as I watched Oswald and Ellen heap the clothes into the dryer, and then sit, side by side on one of the Formica benches, and share a cigarette from Oswald's crumpled pack, I felt like a dead man. I felt that anything I said to them would sound hollow and wrong. I felt she didn't love me any more and I didn't blame her. I went back to the car, and, when she and Oswald emerged (Ellen carrying the bag) I let them drive off without following. If she wanted to phone me she would. The booze was wearing off too. I felt old and ugly and tired.

I groped for the seat belt and my hand came up against something soft. On picking it up, I discovered it was a tissue-paper parcel. Green tissue paper. On the front, in handwriting that was by now becoming depressingly familiar, was written:

TO MARTIN STEEL!

from

A FRIEND!

Inside was another layer of tissue paper. And inside that were two more. Finally, in the middle of the parcel was a piece of paper screwed up into a small ball. I spread it out on the dashboard, and, in the light of the sodium lamps I read:

Dear Martin,

 YOU SHOULD LOCK YOUR CAR!

  You always leave the side-door open on the left-hand side. This is just one of the many interesting facts I know about you. Other facts include:

1. Eating off other people's plates.
2. Making a curious snorting noise at the back of your throat.
3. Thinking you have cancer.

Do not follow Oswald. It is melodramatic. It is the kind of thing that would happen in a book. Not to put too fine a point on it—the kind of thing that might happen in one of your books. But it does not belong to Real Life.

You must rid yourself of the idea that you are INVISIBLE. You can see into the launderette, but we inside can see OUT!! Is this not like life. Ponder this.

Are you having a RETHINK!!!!!!

If you are, here is a course of action that may help you. I suggest you come, next Wednesday at 8 p.m.

To the following address:

> Flat 2,
> 40 St Mark's Road,
> W.10.

P.S.   Wear some *nice* clothes.

P.P.S.   Have you discovered your crime yet?

No, lady, but I may have discovered yours. And who the hell lives at 40 St Mark's Road? And what's all that crap about "rethink"? See you Wednesday maybe, Ellen. Fun fun fun.

13

Midday Monday

It's an extraordinary release. Now I've finally made the decision, and not felt the need to slip back, now I know where I'm going, I feel almost cheerful. Full of intent. The way I was last week must have been some kind of purgative experience, similar to the one I experienced with Julie, and it does look as if only a nasty blow in the crotch will really get me writing. And (this is rather encouraging for one who does want to be a writer) I must be living through and absorbing experience at a faster and faster rate. It took me seven years to pluck up the courage to write about Julie—it's taken me a week to get stuck into Ellen. Perhaps I'll end up like a guy I once saw in the Gents of the King's Arms, Hatfield, who was pouring a pint of light ale down his gullet *while* peeing. The perfect image of the writer's life. In at one end, out the other, at great personal expense. Yes—I've had a rethink, but not of the sort she intended. I'm taking out an option on her life too.

Into this journal will go her life—our life together, and, when the time is right, when the stuff has been processed, it can be tacked on to the Stephen/Julie book. About that, I am now enthusiastic. I just read it through again and it *is* good—despite my moment of doubt, I am firmly back in the chair. How can my artistic method fail? Notebook/journal records the truth—then off the production line, a dash of good writing, amusing location, convincing dialogue and so on, and we have a humdinger of a novel. I'm a factory now. A one-man novel factory. I just hope nothing *else* happens to me, or the thing'll become so big I won't be able to get it out of the study!

The novel I shall write (I'm already re-designing the dust-jacket) will put Ellen, Julie and me in complete perspective. Not vengeful, but austere, and as harsh as truth. A dignified saga of at least a hundred thousand words. Most of the Julie stuff I can use as is, with a little smartening up here and there, and, at the end of Part One I will show the Stephen character realising the essential shallowness of his relationship with Julie and setting out once again, to find something perfect and unpolluted. My narrator, the wise old Mr Judge, has now moved from the club, and his story is told to a slightly different audience. This time, they've grown slightly hostile, slightly common. They interrupt. There's a parallel between the slow descent of the story, and the way I shall use atmosphere. Stephen moves from the College to a city, its name isn't specified, but we know that it's too large and too dirty for comfort. The currency is not stable. There are prostitutes around. He has somehow to get a job, and survive. (Poss. Don't make this *obvious* as from life—Young Man Down From Oxford Getting to Know the Big City, but vague, sinister and shadowy.) Perhaps The City has a series of tests, a complicated set of rules. Gradually as the narrative proceeds, and the interjections become more frequent we get a closer idea of where this second section is set. (A Bomb Site? Something urban and desolate anyway.) So. In the course of these tests, Stephen meets a girl, fair-haired, smiling, who knows all the ways of the City. She's tall with blonde hair. She too has been to College.

The second half of the book is the story of a lad locked in conflict with a woman determined to be as cool as he is, and her eventual total failure to phase him. She will write him notes, put spiders under his bed, and cackle outside his door—all to no avail. He perceives (after some soul-searching) that all she is doing is carrying on the game of their marriage to its logical conclusion, and, if he doesn't act quickly and firmly, they won't be able to break the deadlock. He does, in the end, act firmly and decisively, and, in general, behaves in a far more adult and mature fashion than his wife and his rather unsavoury, inefficient friend, or rather *former* friend.

This is the one. The book to make every man who married a

liberated woman feel better. And, sifting through my memories, I find I can argue quite a convincing case. That's really what I was leading up to last week. And, when I said it wouldn't be a revenge book I didn't mean that it wouldn't be a bitter book; but not the jejune re-created adolescent bitterness of my feeling for Julie, but a three-star, male menopause, cheated-out-of-life bitterness—a great scream of despair that'll make Baudelaire look like P. G. Wodehouse. And I *can* find the case for it.

After that first meeting in Bush House, I paused a while. For reasons which I won't go into here I wasn't at all attracted by the idea of a new relationship at the time. I'd virtually decided on the life of a plainclothes monk, a man mixing in Society and yet not of it. But there's no doubt that I was sexually drawn to her—part of the reason I phoned her was to stop Carter getting his greasy little hands on any part of her anatomy. He spent the days after the racialism incident staring out of the window and muttering to himself about her bum. I seem to recall that, at the time, he was working on a programme about the building of a bridge in Sierra Leone, a place Carter had trouble finding on the map. His task was to cut and edit bits of tape sent back by an exponent of the "verité" school of sound broadcasting, which consists of dropping the microphone at frequent intervals in order to convince the listeners that You Were There. Gradually, we heard less and less of Sierra Leone and more and more of Ellen and her bum. When the ratio was about ninety per cent Ellen's bum and ten per cent Sierra Leone, I put him out of his misery. I phoned her up and asked her out to the cinema.

"Hi!"

"Hullo!"

Cautious voice.

"It's me—Martin Steel."

"Hullo, Martin."

Couldn't quite place me.

"I'm the one at the end of the corridor. With the hump."

"And the glasses?"

"Yes. And the waxed moustache."

"*And* the waxed moustache. And the wig?"

105

"The wig, yes. The wig. That's me."

I was getting into the swing of this. Carter was opposite grimacing enthusiastically and making pumping movements with his right elbow. I waved him into silence.

"At first," she said, "I thought you were the guy with the hump and glasses but with*out* the waxed moustache.

"Oh, he's a dead loss," I said, "racialist."

Carter started to thump the table.

"Cinema next Tuesday?" I said, keeping it bright and brittle.

"No," she said, keeping it even more bright and brittle.

"Drink tomorrow," I said.

"Fine. 6.30 in the Nelson. See you there. Oh, and tell your friend to stop doing that in the office. He'll go blind."

Carter, who was leaning over my shoulder, caught the last remark. In a reasonable mock-up of Insect Death (one of our star tableaux) he swayed and fell heavily to the floor, his arms and legs making short, whirring movements, until they came to rest, stiffly, pointing at the sky. He married a girl called Alice a few months after this, since when no one has seen or heard of him.

The next evening, in the pub, a gloomy place in Trafalgar Square, Ellen and I sat over drinks and got on with it—the romantic foreplay these intelligent women go in for.

Her: So what do you think a relationship should be then?

Me (making it up as I go along): Well, I suppose ... two people who ... (I look at nails) ... who want to be with each other ... and ...

Her (sipping tomato juice): And what?

Me: Well, you know ... there's sexual attraction.

Her: *Right*.

The fact of the matter is this. Men have not a clue about Relationships. They don't want to *know* about Relationships. They want a fuck and someone to take to parties and someone to talk to but they don't know why. And they certainly don't want to spend hours talking about it. What Ellen did was to spend so long defining our attitude to each other that there was (and is) no way out of the maze except by the same ghastly verbal gymnastics that got us in there in the first place.

We got into that maze very gradually and at each stage she was leading me by the hand—a little further in, a little further in. The game consisted of saying "How much do you care?" and getting me to bump up my stake in the proceedings. If I put a quid in, she put a quid in. But the person who always raised the question of money was her—I just wanted to drift along aimlessly, but at every stage she presented me with a kind of Executive Puzzle— do this and we're better—*it's* better, "It" being the relationship. Oh yes, I have things to say about this.

After that first meeting and a tentative kiss outside the Electric Cinema in the Portobello Road there was, of course, the first fuck, which I won't bore myself by describing except to record that it was very nice thank you. After the first fuck, there was an insane week of rutting in locations as far apart as my parents' kitchen (they were asleep at the time), a station lavatory and her bedsitter. All the time, of course, there was conversation, and the steady pressure towards Deciding What We Felt About Each Other. But the first real nasty came after about two months, when I got a flat just down the road from her. With, as it happens, Oswald, but I won't go into how Oswald and I got the flat or how Oswald broke the window, the mirror and the glasses with his Olympic Pro-Model Frisbee.

I got the flat, kissed good-bye to my parents, and, for about two weeks, everything was fine. Then, one cold night in February, we were sitting talking (it was a Sunday night) and I said:

"Bedtime."

"Fine," said Ellen, starting to take off her coat.

"Look, love," I said, "it's Sunday."

"*Yeah?*"

"And I'm knackered."

"I won't hold it against you loverboy," said Ellen, starting to unzip her jeans.

"No," I said, "that isn't it."

"What's it?" said Ellen.

"*Well.* I'd just like to—"

"To what?"

"To sleep alone tonight."

"What on earth for?" said Ellen.

"I just would."

"But—"

"Darling, the bed's very narrow and I just have to be at work early in the morning and I just rather would."

"Oh."

She looked at me. Didn't understand at all. Then:

"O.K."

She started to zip up her jeans. I felt that awful, sudden sadness I often got with her in those days. Not pity exactly, but just a feeling that the world shouldn't be like that. That there shouldn't be any misery. I suppose I felt that because I could see how happy she could be.

"I'll go then."

A real tear-jerker.

"No no," I said. "No, don't. Stay. I mean—stay."

"No no. It's all right."

She did her Broken Doll Being Put Away For The Night routine. Trying to keep my voice calm and rational I said:

"Look stay. I've got a Li-lo anyway."

"Oh great," she said, "that's really nice of you."

"You'll find it quite comfortable," I said protectively.

"*I'll* feel quite comfortable."

"Yeah."

"I'm getting the Li-lo am I?"

"Er—"

Is there no pleasing women? I thought. I didn't want her to bloody stay in the first place. Having graciously given her permission I now get the privilege of being walked all over.

"*I'll* sleep on the Li-lo," I said.

"No no," said Ellen, "I will."

And she meant it. She wasn't going to give up a chance like that. The sight of the tip of her nose peeping over the edge of the sleeping bag still haunts me—that and the shrill, ladylike snore she sometimes falls into when deeply asleep.

Brilliant don't you agree? This whole business of Defining Our Relationship was carried out with the skill and precision of the

108

Wehrmacht moving into Poland. An elaborate game. A game that allowed her to say, on the rare occasions when she lost a point, "It's only a game", but also allowed her to capitalise on all victories as if they were real. More and more emotional money in the bank with every week that passed, more and more the network of private jokes and obligations, with me following every sign like a bored monkey. A trap lads. The modern marriage trap works much as its predecessors—only nowadays you have to love them for it—you have to swear allegiance on the altar of femininity, and confess your past mistakes as if you were being purged by a Party Commissioner.

Oh this is going to be quite a novel. I need a name for Ellen though...

Jackie?

Marjorie?

Mary?

Mary. Not a bad name. Oh the ideas for chapter headings roll off the presses. Lunchtime. Well deserved.

Lunch in this place now involves sorting through penicillin-ridden bits of cheese. The fridge is malfunctioning and I can't seem to get it to work. Ellen usually coped with it alarmingly well. I could, I suppose, go round the corner, but as I seem to have mislaid my key that would involve at least two hours of detailed search. To add to my misery, the lollipop van has drawn up opposite, and is playing the first thirty-four seconds of Popeye the Sailorman arranged for Ice-cream Van by Karl Heinz Stockhausen, two West Indian children are hitting each other with bits of lead piping in the garden opposite, and the fourteenth police siren of the day has just headed down into Brixton town centre. I think they only do it to put the fear of God into the black population.

Maybe I could get someone in to clean? It's fairly obvious that this battle with Ellen is going to last some weeks. I'm sure a decently servile Irishwoman could be persuaded to look after me for a few shillings an hour. Memo to self: WRITE CARD TO NEWSAGENT!

I'll do without lunch. The sink is full of dishes anyway. If I go across to the pub at five thirty, I can get a sandwich. That involves breaking at about four, to allow an hour and a half for Key Tracing. I've suddenly seen it. There's no need to change a thing. Just write it out as it happened. Life with the proper slant and proper plot and I'll nail both of the bitches together. More more more.

14

1 p.m.

There's always been an off-stage conspiracy going on in my life. First inside Julie's head *vis-à-vis* me and Derek, and then inside Ellen's head *vis-à-vis* me. If women can't play you off against someone else, they play you against the machine, pinball fashion, and worse luck if you don't come up to standard. To continue a rather unsuitable metaphor—I never even made the replay.

After she'd established as of right that she spent the night at the flat with me (not to mention Oswald), she then began to complain of the inadequacy of her own living accommodation. This was not unreasonable. At the time she was living in a two-room k. and b. effort near Liverpool Street Station, which consisted of three doors giving on to a landing, used as a thoroughfare by drunks of the parish to and from an unseen but audible lavatory on the second floor. Each door had to be locked every time you went into another room, otherwise, on your return from bath or kitchen, you found many items of electrical equipment mysteriously absent. Two of the doors needed different keys. Consequently, leaving the sitting-room for, shall we say, a cup of tea in the kitchen followed by a bath, involved packing as for a two-week holiday abroad.

The other feature of the flat was its furniture which, at a guess, the landlord had picked up cheap from the set of *Throne of Fear* starring Vincent Price, directed by Roger Corman. The chairs would have fitted snugly into a baronial hall of anything beyond cricket-pitch size—in Ellen's living-room they were like marooned sea monsters, sinister and shadowy.

Gradually, Steel was manoeuvred back there more and more, while Oswald, at the time under similar attack from a girl called Delitha, spent much time in Hammersmith. It was time for Ellen to move into the clinch. She began, carefully and deliberately, to leave items of clothing at my flat, a toothbrush, a bra or a handbag, and, at the same time, to trap me into leaving jerseys and books at the House of Usher, as we had jokily named her place. It was a nice operation, scheduled over two or three months, and bringing with it a new load of habits and traditions. (Note: women create habits in men. This is to their advantage. Not only can they then predict what men will do, they can also, in an emergency, accuse them of being boring and dependent.)

When the habit was fully established, she started to say things like "*Damn*, I've left my hairbrush over at your place," whereas earlier she probably would not have commented. And then things like "It's really stupid, you know, having two places. Don't you think?" Brilliant. She said this as if the thought had only just occurred to her; only the trained eye could see that it was part of the ploy. But, as with the affection thing, it was impossible to fault. If I had said "Oh bollocks you forgot your hairbrush. It is all part of a ploy," she could say "Actually I do want to move in with you, but for a perfectly rational reason. It is *purely* to do with where I put my toothbrush. It is nothing to do with what I feel for you or with—"

But she never used the word marriage either. Another feature of the game. If marriage was discussed at all it was after I had introduced it into the conversation, freaked out by its unspoken presence twenty-four hours of the day. And she always took great care to discuss it at a theoretical level.

"Oh I think marriage is completely irrelevant."

"You do?"

Does she? Why is she saying this?

"Yes. If you love someone you want to be with them."

"Oh. Right."

Do I love her? I'm with her and she's just said that if you love someone

112

you'll want to be with them. So I must be in love with her!!!

"To me," Ellen would say sharply, "marriage only means what you want it to mean."

"Oh sure. *Sure.*"

The thing was—I never even wanted to think about marriage. But, once it had been introduced into the discussion, you had to admit that her ideas on the subject were impeccable. She'd obviously been thinking about it a lot.

And then, I think one Christmas, the crowning touch of pathos. Better than the Li-lo, better than the suitcases and carrier bags she took with her everywhere, better even than the Teddy Bear With A Mind Of Its Own, kept permanently by her side. Better, if such a thing be possible, than the going to bed before me and falling asleep with the light on and her thumb in her mouth. Better thought out.

I came back one day to the flat from a seminar held at the BBC with the pleasing title of "To Whom Are We Broadcasting?" and, exhausted, lay on the bed. When you thought about it carefully, the bed was another touch of pathos—she'd acquired the (feather) mattress from an elderly rouée of her acquaintance named Stephanie—a woman of around sixty, thin as a rake, dying of pernicious anaemia and still managing to get through two bottles of sherry, a few more acquaintances and at least one pheasant a day. A grand woman, really, connecting Ellen to a whole tradition of groovy spinsters. *But*, there I was, lying on the bed, when I noticed, peeping out from under the carpet, the edge of a magazine.

Perhaps, before completing this story, I should say a word about the bedroom. The bedroom was subject to dust storms and to the sirocco of the East End, that blows twelve months a year, and is made up of fag-ends, station-grime, old clothes and Dutch Elm disease. There was damp on the ceiling, insects-a-plenty in the woodwork and we hadn't had the heart to put up shelves, pictures, or anything that made it look like ours. O.K. That was the bedroom.

I was vaguely uneasy at the sight of the magazine. Perhaps because, when at preparatory school, a friend of mine and I secreted a copy of *Health and Efficiency* under the carpet in his room, where it was duly discovered by his mother, who had a Serious Talk with us both. Had Ellen taken to pornography, I wondered, as I reached for the cover. Pornography, but of a different breed. The magazine was called *Homes and Living*. I opened it. There were elegant rooms with beautiful couples seated on black sofas. Ladies in chiffon dresses stood at casement windows looking out over garden space designed by their architect husbands. Relatively unknown television actors were seen seated at pine tables, grinning. Next to the pictures, countless useful details—where the carpets came from, where the curtains were printed, and, below that, shy and practical information about the cost of it all.

I very nearly cried. What can you do against a woman like that? Nothing obvious. She doesn't say "Shall we move into somewhere nicer, *dear*?" She doesn't allow herself to be seen reading *Homes and Living*—an activity that might well expose her to ridicule. *She buys a copy of the magazine, hides it under a carpet and waits for me to find it!!* The mind of a Grand Master at chess, and the body of a sixteen-year-old girl. I always said it.

I sat for some time looking at the pictures. Then I put the magazine back under the carpet. I went into the other room, and waited in the shadows until I heard her key in the lock. Stump stump up the stairs. She came in, palefaced in the dark, and turned to me:

"Oh. It's you."

"Yeah. I got back early."

"Hullo."

"Hullo."

She put her bags down. Didn't turn on the light. Not yet. I looked at her face—smooth oval, lips sculpted into the face.

"Darling—"

"Ye-es."

"Shall we . . . buy somewhere?"

"Uh?"

She hadn't been expecting this.

114

"Get a flat, I mean."

"Well—"

She looked at the floor. Then a nice look, a look of friendship and gratitude.

"We could."

A pause.

"Why not?"

Oh that old deception. But it isn't deception. Shit. I can still be held by it, and, even now, making up accounts, tracing out exactly how she trapped me and the games she used, I still stop, catch my breath and realise I still love her, the way I loved Julie, a hopeless, unsatisfied, adolescent love that I can never confess or explain. Oh damn her. Damn all of them. Damn any explaining of them. I do miss her so much.

A bad lapse. Style is the man I keep telling myself. And, if a bitchy paranoia creates my style, then a paraonoid bitch I must be. All for Art eh? Style should be the final, the ultimate truth behind all your remarks, somehow the best and fullest statement of what you want to say. And these lapses into sentiment do my style no good at all—the long-weekend of cynicism I suppose. My mind in the gutter and my body carrying me upwards towards the skies, True Love and Neoplatonism. I want to be the Great Disdainer and I end up writing like a lovesick girl, unsifted in these perilous circumstances. But I will do it. I will struggle back up and get that sneer in my voice, the hard tones of the man who is always watching, who can be touched by nothing. I'm the one in the corner, hat well down over the eyes—people keep well away from me (body odour?). *That's* better. Now.

It has started to rain outside. Impartially, upon the yard opposite, and on the roofs and on that dog they leave out in all weathers, bounded by the hopeless fences they build in these parts. I think about the time I have wasted and the things I ought to have done. The gutter opposite is leaking, and the rain beats a regular irritable rhythm on the stone sill below—"Julie Julie Julie Julie". And, as the gap gets wider and the rain heavier— "*Julie*anellen *Julie*anellen Julieannellennn". And then, one remorseless tone, like a television after the station's stopped broadcasting, defying anyone to make any kind of sense. "Ssssssssssh."

15

Ought I to mention in the novel that Ellen left Bush House two weeks after she met me and took up work as a teacher? I never quite knew why she left. We had several long and involved conversations on the subject, but I'm afraid when other people start to tell me their problems, I tend to switch off my mind and think about the next meal. If people are going to solve these things—they'll solve them. As far as I remember Socialism came into it at one point, but I'm not sure where. That would have put me off listening. Not that I'm Right-wing or anything—it's just that whenever people start discussing politics I feel an urge to rush out into the fields and nibble the hedgerows. I'm not even, that awful word, "apolitical". I am quite simply a paid up aesthete, capable of being annoyed or irritated by obvious injustice, but resenting all organised attempts to do anything about it.

Am I though? (Follow basic rule here—any direct statement about myself is liable to, nay, probably, no *will*, contain its opposite.) I was what they call "politically active" at university and have been seen walking down the main streets of London accompanied by many other Left-Wing Persons holding banners with punchy things on them like "U.C.A.T.T. workers in Neasden say Fight The Cuts". I was even slightly wounded at the Grosvenor Square Vietnam Demonstration in 1968. I was running for the coach that was scheduled to take me and seventy-five other young socialist hopefuls to that venue when I tripped over the Dean's poodle and broke my nose. I have been known, at dinner parties, to assault people on suspicion of their possessing South African produce. I do, up to a point, *believe* in all these things. But I am also capable of believing the contrary. I have always thought that the ability to hold conflicting opinions is what distinguishes man from the animals, that in its turn is probably a belief in Art or something equally vague. And Ellen thinks Art is something seven-year-olds do on wet afternoons.

The thing that pisses me off about my revolutionary friends (I have six) is not their politics but their crusading, vegetarian zeal and their total lack of contact with workers of any description. Some of them belong to something called the International Socialists, a sort of middle-class club, at whose meetings the ratio of intellectuals to workers is about three hundred to one. By the law of self-justifying minorities, the resultant tendency is a sort of crooning idolatry of said one worker by the ten middle-class platform speakers. It induces in me the sort of numb horror that goes with watching people being lionised. The only bearable Left-wingers I meet belong to the Communist Party, but sooner or later we get on to Czechoslovakia or Hungary or some other place I've never been to, and suddenly everyone gets very angry with everyone else. To cope with this situation, at political gatherings (I have been to three), I describe myself as Anarcho-Liberal-Syndicalist, which usually sends them scurrying to the Penguin Dictionary of the Left, or some similar tome, in order to find out my attitude to Workers' Control, Portugal, Chile, etc. While they are leafing through its pages (usually stopping to bone up on Aid, Althusser, Armaments and Anti-Comintern Agents, liquidation of by Stalin), I make my escape to another part of the room.

Also, does the fact that Ellen is "political" make any difference? I suppose it accounts for her firm grasp of moral priorities, and, partly, for her inability to take me seriously. She's out there in the middle of Real Life. For instance. There's a child in her class of sinned-against tinies, somewhere up there in North London, called Aziz. A quiet, Indian child, very small hands and feet. Always smiling. Sometimes, in the middle of Sand and Water sessions, or Let's Draw a Picture of a Roman Soldier sessions, Aziz will disappear. Ellen looks for Aziz. Is he in the corridor? Has he left the school? No.

Aziz is under his desk. Smiling.

And Jacson. Jacson Ennis the West Indian Child Who Stole
The Bean Bags.

Ellen: Jacson.
Jacson: Yes, miss.
Ellen: What have you got under your jersey?
Jacson: Nothing, miss.
Ellen: Come *on*, Jacson.
Jacson: Bean Bags, miss.
Ellen: How many Bean Bags, Jacson?

Pause.

Jacson: Some, miss.
Ellen: Where were you taking them, Jacson?
Jacson: Home, miss.

Pause.

          Home.
Ellen: *Why*, Jacson?
Jacson: I like them, miss.

It is difficult I suppose for her to take the business of aesthetics
very seriously. Once I remember her telling me about a boy in
her class. This kid had built a makeshift house in one of the
corridors, out of tarpaulin and old, broken-up desks. When they
found that that was where he was going in his lunch breaks,
School Security went in after him. They found he'd been taking
his dinner in there every day, even bringing things from home.
He'd shat all over the floor too. He was cowering in the corner, in
the shadows Ellen told me, too frightened to speak. It was only
then they found out that his mother was an alcoholic, the old man
was out at night work, and every night this kid (I think he was
five or six) had to make himself a meal, get to bed, the lot. Oh
awful things she tells me about.

But then, higher up the ladder, some superior is assessing us—
"Oh *tragic*." "Oh very sad." And we have, as far as possible, to
give an account of ourselves first, for, in speaking of others'
concerns we have to remember that our own are never very far
away. She wouldn't agree with any of this. For her, something is
either useful or it isn't. Simple.

But she can afford to put life before art. Anyone who practises the art of living as she does—doesn't need a substitute. What amazes me, when I come to consider the way she worked on me, is how smoothly the transitions between spontaneity and skilful manipulations are worked.

Possible title for the new work—*The Two Women In His Life*. Needs work.

After we moved out of the House of Usher, she found us a flat and we bought it. We approached mortgage companies (note the first person plural here).

"And tell me, Martin—does your fyansay work?"

"She does, yes."

"And when do you intend getting married?"

"*Ur*—"

"Got you to name the day, has she?"

Oh she was practically dressing me in the mornings, I wanted to scream at the weasel-faced broker who asked me these questions. Together we visited the trendy furnishing shops. How, I wondered, as denim and corduroy simulacra of ourselves wandered past the fish-smokers, steel knives and Continental quilts, can a society support so many obviously inessential people? And not only support them but provide them with a bleeding *shop* in every single major city for them and their tiny denim and corduroy children! And why is it that all of the women have done exactly the same thing to the men? They haven't exactly castrated them, but, by thousands of rational conversations à la Ellen, turned them all into brothers, fellow-conspirators in good living, part of the great web of Unisex. Urgh!

But I went, like so many other P.R. men, journalists and accountants-pretending-not-to-be-accountants of my generation. And, every week, we came back with *more* things. One week it was a table. The next week a chopping block. The week after that—several large jars, of the kind discovered in pre-historic Crete. Until, one day, when the flat was piled up high with dark brown serviettes, glass tabletops and cane chairs, Ellen said:

"We need somewhere a bit bigger."

Notice, you see, how bold she had grown. Now, in my rôle as male collaborator and eunuch, I could be "talked to rationally", i.e. bullied. "We need somewhere a bit bigger." "Too right we do," I felt like replying, "and I can tell you why. The reason we 'need somewhere a bit bigger' is that you have spent at least two hundred woman-hours dragging me round that loathsome shop, looking for yet more restrained and impractical items of equipment. I'll tell you where we'll go and live. Let's go and live in the furniture department of the bloody shop. There are tables and chairs there. There are sofas and beds. There are people like us. I'm sure with the help of an Access card and a little personal charm, it would not be difficult to manage. Or, better still, you go and live in the furniture department and I will go and live in the Saloon Bar of the Hope and Anchor, Acre Lane, Brixton, S.W.2."

I did not, however, say this. What I *said* was:

"O.K., love. Fine."

A word cluster I had begun to use more and more frequently in rational conversations with Ellen. We looked for "somewhere bigger". Tall Victorian houses set well back from the road were found wanting. We trudged round establishments in Acton populated by thirty or forty illegal immigrants, four and five to a room. In these houses, a gas-stove on every landing, a huge, blank wall at the side and sad neglected gardens, Ellen and I behaved like polite sociologists—"Oh really?" or "Is that right?" we'd say as their owners told us long and involved stories about why they were selling the place. But, I wondered as we trudged, what the hell would we do with all these rooms and all these gas-stoves? Would we run up and down the stairs, naked, giggling to ourselves about the housing shortage? Ellen kept saying things like "This'd do for my room." Would we never see each other again when we moved into "somewhere bigger"? Or would it be like those Hollywood films where He and She, both in monogrammed dressing-gowns, kiss goodnight and then stride off to separate ends of the house to sleep?

Eventually, we found this place. "Now," said the taxi-driver who brought us here, "in Brixton you got a mixture. Right? That lowers the price." So Brixton got us as well. We bought even more cane chairs and wall calendars and plastic aprons with reproductions of Goya on them. And I thought to myself, "Well. You've got a house. You've got more furniture than you'll ever sit on. You might as well get married."

Which brought Ellen and me to the conversation in Hyde Park, earlier described. And the Affair itself.

The wedding could not have provided a more striking contrast to Derek and Julie's ceremony. Ellen's mother lives in Wakefield and the grisly ritual was pronounced over us at a register office in that undistinguished city. The building, got up like a public lavatory, did not help. When the last words had been spoken, Ellen and I were staring ahead of us, shellshocked with horror, and the registrar leaned across the desk and said, in a creepy voice:

"That's it. You're married now."

His sidekick, a grubby little man, beamed at us:

"You can kiss her now, you know!"

He said this as if it was likely to be the first time ever. I felt as if my sexual potency had been publicly threatened. In order not to disappoint the little man, Ellen and I went into the longest and strongest Screen Kiss the Wakefield Register Office had ever seen. Behind me, Ellen's mother, all seventeen stone of her, wobbled, like a jelly newly brought to the table.

The main attraction, though, was Oswald. He was supposed to be best man and I had given him careful directions over the phone, an Ordnance Survey map of the area, and several briefings designed to ram home the fact that, for once, he was supposed to be a prop and a support. I thought about hiring the A.A. to make sure he got there, which as it turned out, would have been a smooth move. An atavistic urge led Oswald to Coventry instead of Wakefield. He hung around the register office in his shabby morning suit, eyeing up potential wedding parties to join. In the end, he was moved on, on suspicion of being a pervert. He arrived at the reception four hours late, where he made an inspiring and amusing speech on the subject of Geography.

She married me for the money really. Oh yes. No doubt about it. Her father used to be a miner, and her mother, after he fell several hundred feet down a lift shaft, opened a chip shop, and where she got the money for *that* I don't know because it can't have been all from the compensation. She (Ellen that is, not her mother) sees our marriage as an extension of the class war, an attempt to start an independent dictatorship of the proletariat— her over me, and, just because her family have fashionable Northern vowels and were involved in trendy bits of history like the General Strike, she somehow thinks she's better than me. I can remember a discussion with her and la Jackson senior on the subject of working-class history. I keep telling her that there is no such thing and that history is the history of Top People—but she will come back with the General Strike and the Durham Lock-Out and thousands of other obscure non-events, with which I am not familiar. I feel quite fond of Ellen's mother actually, and, in argument, prefer her style to the bitch fury perfected by her daughter.

Mrs Jackson: Eee, Martin, yer a nice lad really but yer *clue*less. Yer've got good *inst*incts. Yer can see certain things clearly but yer've no nouse about politics. I mean these poor people yer get worked up about didn't just arr*ive* there—they're the result of a system.

Ellen: It's called capitalism.

Me (with dignity): I don't believe in "isms".

Mrs Jackson: Yer live in a bleeding "ism". Whether yer like it or not. And till yer sort yerself out that writing of yours won't come to a thing, I tell you that too. (Looks at Ellen) What shall we do with him!

Followed by more of the same. Ellen's mother does actually talk like a T.V. serial about the North, occasionally using phrases like "Eee ba goom" and strange, possibly faked, dialect words. To complete the image, in the early days of our courtship she insisted on cooking us huge meat teas, and telling me I needed "feeding up". The more I think about it the more I think that Ellen's mother was in on Operation Martin from the beginning, not even she has clean hands. When I was gone—out came the

Martini and the avocado pear as she and the neighbours were pissing themselves laughing at the pitiful Southerner and his forthcoming humiliation by a daughter of the tribe. That's it— the whole family thing fits into the way Ellen, as she dragged me nearer and nearer to the altar, and nearer and nearer to the bourgeoisie (*a* house, *a* car and so on), felt able to load all political guilt for the operation on to me. Like all ideologically skilful people, she has the ability to shift her ground faster than those around her; now you see her, now you don't, and when you don't you can bet she's creeping up behind you with a heavyish wooden club.

And here I come to the nub of the question, the climactic scene of betrayal. Because, after the wedding, when we were already on the couchette, rocking and rolling towards Nice, she played her final and deadliest card:

"Martin," she said, as we lay opposite each other, "do you feel any different?"

"Er—"

Pause.

"Yes. Yes, I think I do."

"Oh."

Another pause. The train rumbles and sways. Then—

"I don't."

"Don't you?"

"No."

I thought about this one for some time. Then I said—

"Don't you think it makes any difference—getting married?"

"Not really," she said. Then—"You do, don't you?"

I saw a hoop. I jumped through it.

"Yes. Yes, I suppose I do."

"Mmm. I don't."

On the other side of the hoop, a bath of paraffin, merrily ablaze. Damn damn. She spends four years of her life devoting her not inconsiderable brain and cunning to getting me to marry her, and then turns round and says that she doesn't think that marriage makes any difference. Superb don't you agree? It works something like this—the most wonderful thing in the world that a

124

man can do to a woman is to marry her (the second most wonderful thing is for him to offer to marry her and be turned down, but that's another story). But modern woman, Ms Woman if you like, despises the gesture while still needing it as reassurance, just as she needs to talk about sex, babies and clothes, while affecting to hold all three in contempt. So, what does she do? She gets the man to make the gesture. Then tells him that the gesture is a heap of shit and that he's a fool for making it. In this manner, she not only makes him dependent on her, she makes him worried about being dependent on her. Thus neatly reversing the pre-marriage situation.

And, when she's done that, she effects the personality change described in this journal. She cackles outside his door. She makes faces at him in the dark. She does impressions of him. She talks about his sexual inadequacies to the girls at work. She begins to leave strange notes for him. And, when he is totally trussed, bound hand and foot by mortgage, house, cane chairs, steel knives and storage jars, she runs off with the lodger to Barnet. She does not, however, being a master of sadism, a black belt in the art of marital infighting, stop there. She persuades her lodger friend to meet her husband. She makes absurd arrangements for him to go to houses he does not know, to eat dinner with strangers, possibly foreigners. She watches him through telescopes. She leaves notes in his car. And, when he is thoroughly and totally demoralised, she says words to the effect of "I want a divorce. I would like my share of the house."

But everything in the bleeding house is hers!! I mean I paid for it, but she wanted it. What am I going to do with a glass-fronted dresser and an eye-level grill and a thing that pings when the meat's ready? All I want out of life is a bed, a few paperbacks and an adequate supply of most of the major brands of alcoholic beverage. And so I bow out gracefully, obtain digs in North London. Pick up the shattered pieces of my life.

No. Women start by making you feel inferior to other men. Then, when they've done that and gone off with these other men, reserve women, crack troops of the ball-breaking union, move in and humiliate you in hand to hand combat. When they've finished with you and staked you out on Hendon Aerodrome with a tin of scorpions up your arse, they leave you, taking all your money. Then—the whole process starts all over again. Because what do I do now? After next Wednesday, when I have finally been done to death? I tell you what I do. *I start looking for another bird.*

Or maybe I don't. Maybe it'll be another man. "Gay recluse seeks companion for houseboat. Only genuine replies *please*."

Or maybe I'll develop a new and incredible technique of masturbating. With soap and audio-visual aids.

Or maybe I'll wait and see what happens on Wednesday.

What will happen on Wednesday?

He-elp.

16

Wednesday 12 midnight

Slowly but surely I am catching up with her. Jesus—from where she is, it must be funny to watch me, lumbering my way through clue after clue. It's so hot tonight too—hotter than any other day this month. I can hardly breathe. But I must write this down now, because I think I have reached what dear Hegel would have called a "synthesis". During the morning I've been doing my periodic check through my journal, as well as working at the Julie–Ellen novel and found the journal as guiltily pleasurable as always. What would anyone reading it make of me? I think, I hope—as someone who vacillated from bitchiness to softness, synthesised the two, and came up much as any other graduate of his generation. I wonder whether what we call personality is in fact simply the point at which you stop thinking about someone and decide to describe them instead, and whether our names for things are simply the witnesses to abandoned work. Nobody could name me then—for diaries are living things, slices of life, hating the clear and over-practical decisions of fiction.

Oswald certainly is a slice of life, a great big grubby chunk of life, incapable of being summed up in an epigram or pinned down with an adjective. Perhaps it is he that prompts these reflections. He's here now, sitting in the room on the landing below mine, shouting at the announcer on Thames Television. "Thank you and *Good*night", he keeps saying. Oswald that is—not the announcer. He's rather drunk and he says he's only "allowed" to stay one night.

The amazing thing is—that this introduction of Ellen into the novel has given it a new lease of life. I did a hell of a lot the other day, and really enjoyed writing it—a good sign. I say a hell of a lot. It was actually about two thousand words, and on Monday I had another three hundred and twenty effort. I had, however, the germ of what might be a very good idea for the resolution. My narrator is in some slum in this bloody awful city. Gradually we realise that his earlier pretence at gentility is a front. The sequence in the club is no more than fantasy. In fact (the punchline) *he* is Stephen Jarrett, and the Julie and Ellen characters are both people in his past. The lofty, austere style has been nothing more than a pretence, a way of distancing himself from the emotion. And as the book slides towards a real nightmare conclusion we see that the guy has nothing worked out, he's alone, despised in the bleakest part of my symbolic city, London the bleakest city in the world. Getting back to this new section. At the moment I haven't actually reached the point where she enters. I've altered the location, disposed of my Derek character, and put Stephen in a furnished room (how nice it is to be a novelist and play God). And then, wham-bang, Ellen enters the scene. She has a very strong symbolic weight in the story, for, if Stephen/Julie represent adolescent love, then Ellen stands for the grown-up marriage, the Woman of the World. I've made her a fashion buyer for a big London store, and upgraded her mother and father considerably. The tone of the thing is still, as it was in the opening Julie-and-Stephen stuff, the stuff I did before Ellen left, very bitter, very hard, but that works. And quite a lot of the feelings I found in myself through writing this journal have boiled over into the story. I think it's now at a stage where it needs leaving—maybe for two or three weeks. Partly because I can't really see a way of ending it until I've sorted the Ellen situation out. If she *is* going to leave me for good then by Christ it is going to be a very nasty book indeed. In the meantime? There's always Steel the diarist—the Man Behind The Books, as the critics will say when this document is published after my Nobel Prize and death.

From the beginning though. Cutting out the abortive attempts to hire Irishwomen whose hobby is cleaning. Straight to six o'clock this evening, and me, walking up St Mark's Road, which turned out to be a rather drab street, tucked away to the north-west of Ladbroke Grove tube station. The whole place is dominated by the Westway and, as Cortinas and heavy lorries move on out towards the M4, in the arches beneath the motorway, the kids of the area, mainly black or poor white, kick balls around, shout, scream and generally while away the long evenings that precede adolescent unemployment. The council (or some other well-meaning but ineffective agent of social change) has attempted to relieve the squalor of the place by painting some of the walls in bright, primary colours. Some of them may have been painted by the kids. But it isn't enough. No amount of poster paint can help the place or wipe out the fact that the cunts who own, control and exploit it are all sitting up in Holland Park, two hundred yards away, and complaining about the rates.

One house in ten, however, has been colonised by the smart brigade, and number 40, it transpired, was one of these. There was a large, blue and white number on the door and, as I stood plucking up the courage to ring the bell, I observed a large man at one of the upper windows. He had his back to me but I could tell he was wearing basic denim kit. He was half-way up a chi-chi step-ladder and, dangling from one hand, was what at first I took to be a giant fan, but which closer inspection revealed to be a Venetian blind, of the Oh So Easy It Only Takes Four Hours And Three Broken Ribs To Assemble variety. Ellen and I once bought a ready-to-assemble chair along these lines. "Just Read The Instructions" it said on the outside. Which was fine—only the instructions were in Norwegian.

To get back to this guy on the ladder, for whom I was already beginning to have a sneaking sense of sympathy. His problem, basically, was this. He was holding the Venetian-Blind-To-Be about a third of the way down, using his right hand for the purpose. At the same time he was using his left hand to balance himself. What had happened was that the slats of the *soi-disant* item of furniture had splayed outwards, and there was no way of

129

making the object easily portable, except by relinquishing his left hand's balance function. This—he seemed unkeen to do. He was hunched away from me, facing up to the room like a boxer. Presumably some Habitat Woman was screaming advice at him from the other side of the room.

As I watched he made up his mind. Coiling his body like a giant spring for the effort, he launched upward and outward with his left hand in a desperate bid for the slats. As he did so, however, he toppled forward, and both he and the Oh So Easy To Assemble Venetian Blind headed down towards the floor. It was only then that I recognised him. It was Derek. No one else in the world could fall off a ladder like that.

I looked for signs of structural damage to the house. It wasn't shaking. Then I went and rang the bell of Flat 2. I seriously thought about stealing away quietly towards Ladbroke Grove, but the thought of Ellen kept me at my post. I rang the bell for the second time. Presumably Julie was still reassembling Derek, if it was Julie up there with him. Suddenly, from a panel of speakers at the side of the door there was an aggressive storm of static. In the middle of this explosion, I heard Julie's voice, sounding rather like a BBC correspondent, filing from a very distant part of the globe.

"Hullo!" she said.

"Hi!" I said, and then wheeled round to check that no one had seen me talking to the wall.

"I'll let you in," said Julie's voice. I was half expecting a long arm to glide round the corner of the stairs à la Plastic Man, but in fact, there was only a high pitched whine, and the door, against which I was leaning, suddenly gave way. Magic.

I found myself in a large hall furnished with Coconut Weave Matting and painted a tasteful cream. I stood around waiting for a recorded voice to say "THERE IS AN IN-TRUDER ON THE PRE-MISES! FIND AND DES-TROY! ALL UNITS!" but was disappointed. Instead, around the corner of the first landing, wearing a floor-length gown of apparently Indian design, drifted none other than Julie. She paused at the head of the stairs. I half expected her to scream or faint or snarl, but she did none of these things.

"Martin—" she said, "oh good."

I clicked up the stairs towards her, trying to look as if I had expected this. When I got up to her level, she laid her head on one side and stared, fishy-eyed over my left shoulder. Oh God! She wanted me to kiss her. I gave her a peck on the cheek and (a new gesture this) she took my arm and led me towards her front door. Had she taken up Yoga? There was a dreadful calm about her. I tried to stop myself grinning with fear and started some nonsense about how fascinating the area was.

In the front room, Derek was kneeling on the floor in the middle of what was once going to be a Venetian Blind. He looked up as we entered, and scrambled, boyishly, to his feet. He looked very tanned, and about four years younger than when I had last seen him. But his hands were still the same size.

"Hi!" he said, in a calm and relaxed way. Had he taken up Yoga as well?

"Derek—" said Julie, "can you cope with drinks? And I'll just—finish off in here."

"Fine, love," said Derek.

It was all very amazing. Here they were—both wearing perfectly adult clothes and talking to each other much as Ellen and I did. I hadn't counted on this. If I expected to see Derek ever again, it was wearing a donkey jacket, and that same helpless, giant's grin. But this person wasn't Derek. This person was, admittedly, rather above normal human size. But he looked *almost normal*. And it was quite impossible to guess what he was thinking. He might even be a success. A cold sweat broke out on the back of my neck.

"It's a real drag Ellen couldn't make it," said Derek, pouring me a colossal Scotch.

"Isn't it?" I said. So he knew Ellen as well, did he? Possibly the four of them were planning to go away together, leaving me the house in Brixton and the flat in Ladbroke Grove. Was this part of an elaborate revenge ceremony for what I'd done to him all those years ago? I sat on a huge sofa, that had Access Card written all over it, and waited for him to make the next move. He did not reach for a carving knife or press his face close to mine and snarl

131

in a sinister fashion. Instead he sat down on a large bean bag opposite to me and said—

"How's things?"

"Fine," I said, "did Ellen—er—"

"Still at the Beeb?"

"Ur—"

Were they keeping a file on me?

"Er—yes—actually. And you?"

Julie appeared at the door, one hand on the doorjamb. She looked as if she'd just had a Badedas bath and was waiting for something to happen.

"Derek's in Community Law."

"*Really!*" I said.

I looked at him, grinning up at me from his bean bag. Community Law, eh. A groovy way of saying he was a solicitor I supposed. He certainly didn't look like a solicitor. He looked like a professional surfer.

"Yeah," said Derek, "up in the Grove."

"Ah."

Julie, with the assurance of a practised hostess, steered the three of us towards the dinner table. The frustrating thing was—although I was dying to know how Julie knew Ellen and what Ellen had said on the phone and whether there was any chance at all of her turning up, I didn't dare risk my cool by so much as mentioning her. Luckily Julie started doing my work for me.

"It's weird," she said, "because although I haven't seen Ellen for ages not for ages have I Derek? I have been in touch you know but it was only this week when she phoned that I realised."

"Realised what?"

"About you and her."

"Oh," I said, "you heard."

"Heard what?"

"Nothing. Nothing."

Shit. In other words, Julie had only just heard about Ellen and me being together. She had not yet caught up on the latest development, i.e. that we were separated. It seemed a pity to remove an illusion so recently acquired so I said:

"Pity she couldn't make it."

"I know," said Julie, "we could have had such a lovely chat."

"So you and Ellen were. . . ."

"Right. At school together," said Julie.

"Amazing, isn't it?" said I.

Derek was now well out of the conversation and well into the taramasalata. It was pleasing to note that some things about him had not changed.

"I met her in London just after we came down," Julie went on, "and I hadn't seen her since the sixth form. And we had a drink."

"But didn't discuss mutual friends."

"Right."

"Terrifying really," I said, "how people have an independent existence."

"Oh I think so," said Julie, "you can go for years and years and think that you know someone. But you don't really know them at all."

She gave me a conspiratorial smile. How bleeding true that was, I thought. I was rearranging my universe around the fact that the only two women I had ever loved had been at school together, and that I did not know this, although I was in the process of writing a novel about them both, when Derek said:

"Are you involved on the political front these days?"

"Er—" Perhaps this was the beginning of the Piss Take.

"Er—no," I said.

"Derek's in Radical Alternatives to Prison," said Julie.

"Is that right?"

"And so the conversation slipped between velleities and carefully caught regrets." It was like watching a strip-tease dancer doing the seven veils. I kept my eyes peeled for what both of them had become, what they were really like, but things moved so quickly and we all have so many defences now, that there was no way of knowing. I think, really, that it was what it seemed on the surface, three graduates meeting for a chat about Old Times. The old jokes and the old animosities had become routines that we slipped into gratefully, aware that they had lost their sharpness. Even my habits of thought about Derek, once so

133

violently bitter or curiously tender, had become bland. I forgot everything we discussed but I know that it was reasonably done, and that now they live in my mind not as a couple who betrayed me or hurt me, but simply as two more people I fail totally to understand. Ellen didn't come into the conversation again. Until—

At about ten thirty, Derek had to phone someone about a meeting and went into his study to do it. Julie and I were left alone. Eyeing each other cautiously.

"Well," I said, "this seems O.K."

"Mmm," she said.

"Funny. You knowing Ellen."

"And funny," said Julie, "her ringing me like that."

"Yes," I said.

There was a pause. How much did she know? I didn't much care.

"It's odd," said Julie, "that we never talked about you."

"Yes."

"But even odder because we *did* talk about you but not about *you* if you know what I mean."

"No I don't."

"Well—when I met her in London, I hadn't seen Ellen for ages. And we talked of this and that. And she told me she was living with someone. That was you I suppose. And I told her about how I'd had this awful scene although I didn't say who *with* and I told her about the letters."

"Julie, for God's sake—"

"Oh there was no way she could know it was you. Unless you've told her since. But knowing you—"

"I haven't told her. I mean I told her about you of course but not about the letters. And I know—"

"Don't, Martin. It doesn't matter now. Really."

Then Derek came into the room again and we said our good-byes. We said we'd meet again soon. Of course we would. And Ellen would come round next time. The four of us. It would be perfectly marvellous. Derek was a bit drunk. He slapped me on the back.

134

Then I made my way down into the hall, called out a few last jokes and was out, at the top of the steps, looking out over the street, free at last. Or was I?

17

Are you more honest to a piece of paper than you are to yourself?
Does writing things down change them? Obviously I'm keeping
lots back from this journal. I haven't mentioned the colour of my
hair, my two brothers, my deaf uncle in Henley, my deranged
aunt in Leeds . . . and I haven't so far mentioned what happened
after the Julie thing broke up. Except very casually. Is that
because I'm ashamed of it? Or was frightened that Ellen might
find out. I always remember the story of Boswell entering one of
his amorous escapades in his journal. Unfortunately his wife got
hold of it—the journal I mean. Very embarrassing. And,
although I've kept the journal under lock and key in the bottom
right-hand drawer, it has been a constant fear that, one evening
at dinner, Ellen might casually drop a—

"Er . . . reading something of yours today . . ."

"Yeah?"

"Mmm. A sort of . . . journal . . ."

"Ah."

Gulp gulp. The fact of the matter is I am very ashamed of what
happened. And, previously, I was pretty certain that only a
careful reading of the novel and the journal together could lead
to her finding out. But, if she knows Julie and has read the novel,
she's equally well qualified to put together a Who's Who in
Martin Steel's life. She could quite easily have read the opening
chapters of the novel, realised it was a portrait of Julie, and by a
process of deduction worked out that I was the shit who wrote the
letters. There is an incident in Chapter 3 which draws on some of

that stuff. Before I get on with what happened after I left Julie's I'd better set it all down.

Oh what a tangled web we weave. This situation would never have arisen if I had told Ellen about Julie. Or rather, if I had been honest with Ellen about Julie. For a start, why, when talking about her, did I change her name to Margaret? And invent a different colour hair for her, and a different university? And why do I take an insane delight in making sure all my stories check out? I suppose because I'm a fantasist. I love inventing alternative identities, and I can't stand the idea of anyone knowing everything about me. But given that, why didn't I put this down earlier? This was intended to be a place where I was totally honest with myself, pulled no punches. My *not* putting it down casts a new light on the novel. You see I'm not sure that it was as simple as being afraid that Ellen might find the journal. I think she could have been persuaded that my fictional Julie was an invention pure and simple, and it's a commonplace of fiction that people don't recognise themselves. The person with the funny face or the funny walk is always someone else. No. I deliberately withheld the stuff that happened after I split up with Julie because I wanted to keep some of myself back. In writing you use so much of your personality that it's tempting to keep just a little bit, some secret, from that awful blank page, eating up so many of your secrets. But I always keep the important bits back. Like a kid who loses his nerve on the diving board I say, at the last minute, "No no. I'm frightened. I don't want this."

All of this must have started when I was a kid. I have two brothers, you see—one of them a child of the Fifties, ex-jazz freak, ex-Rock 'n' Roller, ex-driver of ropey American saloons, the other a streamlined I.C.I. executive, on the edge of the disastrous slide towards middle age. They both hate me. Well—they don't exactly *hate* me but they're suspicious of my attempts to carve out a personality for myself. When I was seven or thereabouts, when a dispute arose as to who was to have the last piece of cake, first of all Paul, the eldest, and then Dave, the middle brother, would sit on my chest for ten or fifteen minutes until I turned a light purple.

After this play-off round, Paul would thump Dave and eat the cake. Dave might pick up a couple of crumbs, and, in order to vent his spleen, would sit on me for another five or ten minutes, chewing ostentatiously. I evolved several methods of defence. One was to scream for the nearest adult, usually my mother. This had certain advantages in the short term but in the long term was counter-productive as Dave and Paul were adept at finding places far from the adult world where they could sit on me until the blood came out of my ears. Another was to fight back— virtually impossible as I am built like a praying mantis, and any sign of aggression was met by ruthlessly repressive measures. At the age of eight I could have given Talleyrand lessons in the art of the possible. My alliance system was complicated, a world of betrayals and false affection. I became adept at playing off Paul against Dave, at pretending I didn't want anything they wanted. But I had my secret desire and the desire grew out of the deception and the delicate games with other people.

My secret desire, of course, was to write. And that I did, on the back of my Latin exercise book at school, on spare bits of paper, on the backs of envelopes, on walls even. In my primary-school phase I wrote a short story about frogmen, a poem about an owl and a series of limericks about my maths master. At twelve I was much possessed by death and my imagery was full of skulls and decomposing bodies. At fourteen I wrote nothing but straight pornography, in code, and from fifteen on it was nothing but poetry, mainly addressed to a squat third-former at my school called Beavis. I published it in the school magazine under titles like "Villanelle for H.B." or "Sonnet to a Friend", which caused everyone in the know to leer suggestively every time young Beavis waddled past me on his way to the changing-rooms or the tuck-shop. If Beavis ever read or understood these public proofs of my affection he gave me no sign of it. But it didn't matter. Writing for me had started as a solipsist game, an unscramblable code. It was a release and a retreat not a means of communication. It was a way of escaping when Dave or Paul were belting me or when, later, girls were ignoring me. I can remember the shock and horror I felt when my first creative work was read and judged. It

138

happened like this. I think I was about fourteen at the time. I had a small notebook, containing poetry and prose pieces and, one evening, I foolishly left it on the cover of my bed. On the inside front cover I had written:

"This book belongs to Martin Steel. Undiscovered Poet, Playwright and Genius."

At about nine o'clock I remembered what I'd done, galloped up the stairs to retrieve it only to find, on the inside front cover in my father's unmistakable, Biro-ridden handwriting, the message—

"Well. Undiscovered anyway."

Oh my father my father. I haven't really been very honest about him either, have I? He's a retired accountant, who published a few travel books way back in the Fifties. They were rather good, actually, and for him they were more important than the figures he added up at some office down in the City that I was never allowed to visit. One of my strongest memories is coming back from school, looking up at the front bedroom and seeing him outlined against the window, back bent over his desk, his shoulders twitching as he typed. I don't hate him as I said earlier. I couldn't say exactly what I feel now, when I turn into the driveway of our house on one of my rare visits and I see him up at his desk, in the old position, like a cut-out, a trick person designed to fool burglars. It isn't love—it's too complicated for that. And it isn't indifference or contempt or fear or distrust. It's like ... I don't know what it's like. When I was very small my mother and he used to fight all the time. Once, I remember, he knocked her down the stairs. And then he was a kind, buttoned-up man, taking me to school and telling me a long, involved story about a fire-engine. First he smelt of tobacco, and in our lavatory, after he'd used it, there was a sour, male smell that went with hair under his arms or the doughy whiteness of his arms and chest when I saw him in the bathroom. Then he was a successful dinner-party father, flushed with wine, and making people laugh. None of these impressions is the final truth. I register them, record them and promise myself at some future date to try and understand them. This is the awful thing about starting to tell the truth, as I now am. It goes against the habit of years, the very fact that I am writing it down, keeping it secret, is bound up with my essential duplicity, and yet (I repeat it to keep my courage up) I am I am I am I am trying to tell the truth in the written word where the lying started.

And, while we're at it—my mother. I flick back through the pages of this journal and am horrified at the account I have given of her. Why have I only selected the bizarre, the laughable? She's a once beautiful woman with a tragedy of her own. I remember going into her bedroom (sacred smelling place!) and seeing a photo of a young girl on her bedside table. I'd never seen it before. It was an old photo but in a new frame. I stood looking at this picture, feeling quite incredibly randy, and heard a footfall behind me. My father padded into the room.

"Who's that?" I said.

He looked at me oddly.

"Don't you know, boy?" he asked.

"No. Who is it?"

"Your mother. When she was young."

"She looks nice."

"Yes."

We both looked at the picture for some time. Then we looked at each other. One of us had to leave the room first, and in the end I did, leaving him standing back, looking at the photograph as if he'd never seen it before.

I suppose I'm what psychiatrists would call "mother-fixated"—if peering through the bathroom door to get an eyeful of her changing is mother-fixated. When I was eight you understand. I wouldn't *dream* of doing such a thing these days. My sexual contact with Mater consists of a wet kiss on the cheek every third week and that seems to do me. And there's never been any of the traditional mother/wife conflict between Ellen and Mrs Steel Senior. Lies lies lies Steel stop it (how difficult this truth telling lark is). I remember whenever Ellen and I went out to the cinema the old lady would ring the flat and instruct Oswald to tell her what time I got back, often adding, in hushed, confidential tones, *if* I got back. This caused great agonies of

conscience to the poor lad who is justly famous for being Good
With Parents. Often, whenever the phone rang, Oswald would
leap to his feet and rush out into the street, in order to avoid the
decision-making crisis consequent on such a call. No—I'm a
typical Mummy's boy, looking for first-class hotel service from
every woman I meet, only with rather less involvement than is
customary with hotel staff.

Nothing but honesty now, Steel. She's probably rumbled you
anyway. I might even hand over the manuscript of the novel to
her, cast it on her mercy. O.K., Ellen I'm coming clean:

After I split up with Julie and after we came down to London,
in the period before I met you I was very lonely and pissed off.
And I took to writing...

Letters.

Rather paranoid letters I'm afraid. Started as a joke and got
less like a joke the more of them I wrote. I wrote these letters to a
girl called Julie whom you were at school with but whom you
didn't know I went out with. Why? Because most of what I have
told you about my past life is a heap of bollocks. I mean—not
dramatic lies, but a distortion here, an embroidery there—the
shifting and replacing of anecdotes about various people. I've
told you all the Julie stories but I've divided them up between
different people with different names. This is connected to my
attitude to Art. Yes, Art. I lie to the page the way I lied to you and
I don't like the effect either had which is worse but I'm
stopping now. I swear it. I think when I was small somebody told
me that imagination was making up stories, and I somehow got
hold of the totally erroneous notion that the better a book is the
further it is from reality, or rather that I graft a plot on to a
situation, simply feel the need to crowd the thing with incident.
This can be remedied, though.

Sorry about that. Now about the...

Letters.

Sample:

Deer Miss,
            I saw you undressing last night! What a nice bum you
141

got! One of this days I'll be up you like a rat up a Drain; what an arse!!

> Kiss kiss,
> Big Malc

Or the phone calls:

Julie: Hullo, 856-0214.
Me: Mmmm.
Julie: Hullo!
Me: Mmmmm.
Julie: Who's that?
(I breathe heavily)

I used to go round to the flat in Greenwich, where she was living with Derek, and watch it, hidden in a doorway half-way down the street. I'd see Derek come home from whatever place he was conning money, and then, about half an hour later—Julie. I'd wait till the light went on in the bedroom and then clear off. Sick eh? Another time I put a personal ad in *The Times* for her to ring a north London telephone number. My parents' number. I rang her up from call boxes and left the receiver off the hook. After about six months of this she threatened to get the police onto me. Or, rather, she didn't. Derek phoned me one night, sounding anguished and formal, and said that if this went on they would have no alternative, etcetera.

I only saw her one more time before I met Ellen and that was quite by chance—in the King's Road. I was shopping for a pair of trousers that would radically alter the design of my buttocks without crushing my genitals to pulp, when she stepped out of Safeway's Supermarket and headed down towards Fulham. I ran after her and caught her up outside the Chelsea Drug Store—she wouldn't stop, but walked, fast and self-contained, without looking at me. I poured out a whole stream of stuff—apologies, abuse, incoherent protestations. People were looking at us. She stopped then, turned to me and said in a stiff governessy voice "Martin, let me make one thing very clear. I am not going to talk to you. I am not going to acknowledge your existence until you *grow up*. O.K? And until you do grow up—let me say another thing. You won't amount to anything, not your ideas or your cleverness or any of that until you decide to behave less like a sick schoolboy and more like an adult. O.K?"

A man in a blue corduroy jacket watched us. This was the best free cabaret he'd had in years. Other pedestrians walked either side of us, as if we were a traffic island. I was about two yards from her. I wanted to touch her, to hurt her, to shake out the years I'd wasted on her, but still I couldn't. I can see now how wrong I was. The only way to live with past defeats is to accept them. But oh God why is it so painful and why does it take me so long to come to these Christmas card conclusions!

She seemed sad for a moment. "You ought to see someone," she said, "a doctor or a psychiatrist or someone who could help." Then she walked off through the Saturday morning crowds and I went to a bench in one of the squares between the road and the river, bit my lip, and swore, strangely, to myself.

Well—there was a lot more stuff. You dragged it out of me. Ellen—I'm not a very nice person. The fact of the matter is this— I have an unsavoury, vindictive attitude towards people. A desire to avenge imagined wrongs. Which is why I started writing about Julie. And why I added you. But I promise, Ellen, from now on the novel is going to contain, as well as bitterness, a tender compassion, charity and a kind of noble sadness at the way life has treated me. You've made your point about Julie. You're trying to say "Don't write about her this way. Be calm. Objective. In order to be a good novelist it is essential to be a Good Man. Your moods of bitchiness followed by softness are not creativity at all."

Well—I'm afraid you're wrong there. You see, my talent as a novelist comes out of bitchiness—that's what creates my style— and what makes the novel good is that it's sharp and cruel. That's the source of my talent. But you are right—I could be *better*. Everyone could always be better. Tolstoy could be better. And I think you're right, that if somehow I could comprehend charity as well as bitterness, I'd give the novel another dimension. I continue with the confessional.

143

Anything else I can drag out of the inner recesses of my soul?

Well. . . . I once dropped a tortoise off a railway bridge in Kilburn.

This really is hurting, Ellen.

I was eight at the time. Anything else?

I have lied about my age. I have lied about my sexual conquests. I have lied to you about loving you and not loving you. I'm a worm, honey.

And I have lied about the only other Emotional Event in my life, i.e. Julie.

Reasons:
1. Once you have told a lie it's difficult to go back on it. If I hadn't invented affairs with two other women maybe I wouldn't have lied about Julie.
2. The desire to keep secrets allied to a total inability to keep my trap shut. I sometimes think I'm like a dumb animal that thinks it's camouflaged but isn't.
3. I lie about a lot of things. Purely for fun. And I was a shit to Julie.

Is this enough or do you want more?

I cultivate an air of lovable indecision when I think it may be to my advantage. I borrow money and don't repay it. I've lost the phone bill.

This hurts.

Most of all. I can't make up my mind about anything. I swing round and round like a compass gone crazy, justifying, apologising, blustering, bitching, lying, not lying, not making any kind of sense. You're the only person who makes me make any kind of sense. Without you I'm like a church on a rainy day, like Brazil without Pele. Without you I have about as much personality as a dead budgie. Without you, frankly, I might as well tie a couple of weights to myself and lean a little too far over Hammersmith Bridge.

This journal is a love letter and always has been. It is written for you. No one else but you. It's turning into a begging letter and

144

if you don't come back soon it'll turn into a Doctor's Prescription. Forty sleeping tablets or worse.

Feel better now.

This of course is what she wanted. Quite right too. She reads the novel, is shocked and appalled by its bitterness and the savage and yet compelling way it caricatures an acquaintance of hers. She also realises that the twisted and cynical author of the work could well be the man who persecuted her friend. She needs time to think. And, probably, time to roast me a little. She pushes off. When she thinks I'm liable to be at just the right temperature, she lets me know, in spectacular fashion, that she knows about me and Julie. She knows more about me than I think she knows. Then she leaves me alone again.

She wants to frighten me.

She has. I'm frightened. I'm changing my ways.

I have been unobservant, obsessed with myself, shattered her self-respect. God knows what I've done. And, because she knows me so well—because she can predict almost my every move— she's run this whole thing as a laboratory experiment. The change of attitude towards me. The notes. She's trying to teach me a lesson. Well—I've got the ultimate defence now. I'm going to learn it, swallow it whole like a good boy.

I will never tell another lie. I will love others. I will listen to everything she has to say. A thud from downstairs. What *is* Oswald doing?

I have just been downstairs to check. Oswald was throwing Guinness bottles at Diddy David Hamilton, the Thames Television announcer. I reasoned with him. I told him that Diddy David was not actually inside the television, but in a studio in the Euston Road. If Oswald wanted to throw Guinness bottles at him, he should take a mini-cab up there. In the meantime, I added, he was in danger of breaking one of the last of my links with the outside world. Oswald then suggested phoning Diddy David at the studios. I told him he would only get security guards. "Fine," said Oswald, "I will talk to them."

He set out for the hall, but half-way down the stairs,

changed his mind, or, more probably, forgot where he was going. He is now sitting on the third step down from the landing, chin in hand, brooding over the mess of newspapers, shoes and rubbish bags that I have allowed to accumulate in the hall.

But it is Oswald who will lead me back to Ellen. I'd better get on with what happened when I met him this evening, what he gave me, and how, at last, I see a chance.

18

When I got out of Julie's flat, I stood, looking out over the street, getting the first glimpses of the suspicions I have just described. As I stood there, I heard a voice coming from beyond a wall, fronting a neighbouring garden, about twenty yards down the road.

> I wish I was
> In Carrickfergus.

The voice was that of Oswald, and he was "singing", something Oswald only does when very, very drunk. The sound resembles a German style known as Sprachstimmung and it has the same eery, prehistoric quality as some of Schoenberg's less tuneful compositions. As I listened, Oswald walked into vision, shoulders hunched, and, under his arm, a very tattered copy of what was undoubtedly today's *Daily Mail*. He was wearing his second-best jacket which looks as if it has spent some time at the bottom of a dog-basket. He saw me and waved, converting the wave, at the last moment, to a clenched fist salute.

"Hi!" he said.

"Hi!" I replied. I walked down towards him. To my surprise I was very glad to see him.

"Something really weird has just happened to me," I said.

"Oh really?"

"Mmm."

I didn't try to explain it.

"Mart," said Oswald, "I have had a few. I have shifted a few beers this evening."

"Fair enough," I said.

"Ruddles," said Oswald, sitting on the low garden wall of number 40 and kicking morosely at the pavement, "Ruddles. A very high density beer is Ruddles."

"It is," I said.

"Brakspeare's, Theakston's Old Peculiar, Wadworth's Number Six Brew Made in the Traditional Way for over Two Hundred Years."

He lay full length on the wall, looking up at the sky.

"I have been to a beer festival," he said, "a Real Beer Festival."

"Great, Oswald," I said. "Shall we go?"

"Sure," said Oswald, "I'll drive."

He rolled off the wall and lay on the pavement, still looking up at the stars, high above W.10. It was pleasant standing there. I made no move to pick him up. After a while he said:

"I have a message from your wife."

"Oh. Great."

"She sends me on errands," said Oswald, "errands I do not understand. You are both wonderful people. Very sensitive. Very warm."

"Thanks, Oswald."

No one passed. No one looked out of the window. There was just me and Oswald. He continued:

"Carlsberg Special Brew, however," he said, "is a lager. A Continental Drink. What we call a top-brewed beer."

"Is that right?"

"That is right."

Another restful interlude. Then:

"She said," went on Oswald, "that you would leave this place between 11 and 11.30. And she was right. She knows you, Mart. She knows you well."

"She does indeed."

"I do not know who these people are," went on Oswald, "but you do and she does. And you will meet her again, Martin. You will meet her again."

Then, sinking his head into his neck like a tortoise and folding his arms tight into his side, he rolled smartly towards the gutter,

148

humming in a high-pitched tone, rather in the manner of a top. He stopped on the kerbstone, face down, and looked up at me, slyly.

"I do not like the rôle of Go-Between," he said. "I find it a strain."

"Is that right?" I said.

"I feel odd. It is not pleasant." Then, for about a minute, he became totally sober and completely normal.

"Thing is, Mart. It all started as a joke in a way. And she got more and more manic. And I'm not quite sure what she's up to. And neither is she. But I'm afraid she's going to blow the whole thing."

"What whole thing?"

"I don't know. What she was trying to do. You and her."

"Well, what *was* she trying to do?"

"Like I said the other day. To start with a breathing space or something. But now—" A pause. "I don't know. I just don't know."

He then pushed both arms forward as if about to do a press up and, using the arms as a point of balance, drew up his legs smartly, so that he was crouched like a frog on the pavement. He held this position for a few moments, pulling at his hair.

"It's a sticky one," he said. "I *really* like her actually. *Really* like her."

"I know," I said.

He bounded to his feet and stood at attention, staring straight ahead of himself.

"Where is she, Ossie?"

"To start with we were in Barnet. At a mate of hers. Della Stevens. And now we're holed up in Archway."

"With Jackie?"

"With Jackie."

Six-foot woman's liberationist. Doesn't like me. Once again I pondered the question of how far this was a battle of wits. Perhaps a normal, timorous husband would have rung round all her friends ages ago. Not me. And it was significant that Ellen had moved from a place I didn't know, neutral territory, straight into the camp of the enemy, which, in its turn, was probably why Oswald had come to see me.

It's not only Jackie that's the enemy. I've always had a thing about Archway, all those lonely Cypriot cafés with Coca-Cola signs above them, and women in black shawls cowering behind urns. It was in Archway—just at the bottom of the hill, walking down towards Holloway, that I first realised quite how unattractive I am, physically. I was threading my way through pedestrians, as Crane Freuhauf juggernauts belched smoke out at me, when I caught sight of a tall, thin creature, with a long nose, walking towards me. His feet were turned out like a duck's, and it was obvious that in a few years he would be totally bald; in a way, I thought, it would be a relief for him. He could give up trying.

It was then that I realised that the creature was wearing exactly the same clothes as I was, and it was a short step from there to discovering that it was in fact the mirror image of myself, caught unawares in a shop-window, blazoned out for the crowds—a living proof of my freakishness. I've had it in for Archway ever since.

I could imagine the line Jackie was feeding her: "Basically Martin's a male chauvinist. Oh sure he's learned how to hide it, but this is all part of the male response to pseudo liberal pressure as he feels his penis-centred male ego collapsing round him. Now I'd just like you to strap on this fifteen-foot dildo and we'll rip off a couple of purely clitoral orgasms before the Gateways." Oh every move counts in these games. Thank God I had a card to play, knew vaguely the way things were going.

"I hope I'm doing the right thing," said Oswald.

"I think so," I said.

"She's in a bad way really. *Not* under control."

"No?"

"No."

We looked at each other. Oswald puckered his brow in worry.

"Hope you get it together anyway," he said. And I knew that we wouldn't talk about Ellen again.

I got him into the car. Once safely in the passenger seat, his paper clutched on his knees, peering round himself like a pensioner, he got on to Recitatives. These are prose pieces, delivered in an unconvincing Galway accent, and learned from an elderly Irish sub on Oswald's paper:

When I think of dear old Ireland—
It's the place where I was born.
When I think of those hills those streams those vales
I pant! And ah! I mourn!

He looked out of the window, genuinely moved by his own performance. In fact, Oswald was born in Weybridge, and the nearest he ever gets to the Emerald Isle is Mooney's in the Strand. I met Oswald's father once—he's a fat, jolly man who's done about four years, in various jails, for fraud offences. Somehow or other, he emerges from the prison of the moment and picks up his life—mowing the lawn, serving drinks to neighbours and watching the television in his immaculate Weybridge home with his immaculate Weybridge wife. And no one in Weybridge takes exception to his way of life. No one hisses "jailbird" at him in the golf club. They seem to treat it as an occupational hazard of business.

By the time we reached Kensington, he'd got on to a badly remembered line in Virgil, and, as we crossed the river, it was the Martini jingle. I sang with him, suddenly hopeful.

In some ways the past week or so must have been worse for Oswald than for me or Ellen. Presumably she, like me, has been moving from bravado to desperate insecurity, from feeling quite above things to feeling desperately lonely. But we are both playing the same game we've always played, even if the stakes are a lot higher. Witness my glee at discovering her whereabouts and knowing that she doesn't know I know. Bluff, double bluff, the whole apparatus of our daily life suddenly more desperately real, more like the foreign policy of the ego than ever before.

But I don't think Oswald ever saw any of this going on. If he saw it at all it was as a minor irritation, something he didn't want to believe in. He's always, I suppose, Believed In Us As A Couple. The way people do. We were allowed to have rows, but not rows that threatened his security—they all had to have their origins in simple, explicable phenomena. "Oh sure you're tired" or "It gets like that sometimes." Occasionally I think that the whole of the adult world is made up of people trying to get other people, either in ones or twos, to behave like their parents.

I have now formulated a new policy for the novel. Simply to carry on living through all this, hoping I'll get out alive, keeping my ears and eyes open, planning the book in my mind as we go.

Curiously, Oswald and Ellen and I were a fairly satisfactory *ménage à trois* on the one-child-family basis. I remember when Oswald and I were sharing the flat, Ellen and I were in the middle of what he would call a "spine-shattering fuck" and, by accident, he wandered into the room. The curious thing was that not one of us was in the least embarrassed. Ellen and I agreed that if he'd asked us out for a drink we would have broken off momentarily, said yes or no and then gone back to our work with a will. The first question I ask Ellen or Ellen asks me when we get back in the evenings is:

"Where is he?"

Getting back to the question of how bad it must have been for him last week. This connects up with the Julie thing. Because, really, it's all about understanding that people have separate existences of their own. And while I was worrying about how he could do such a thing to me, presumably he was trying, as hard as he could, to keep the balance between us. Maybe we've always treated Oswald as a mascot rather than someone capable of getting up and walking off on his own.

I *think* he's capable of getting up and walking off on his own.

I remember the first time I met him. It was in a pub in Notting Hill Gate—old-fashioned place with, for some extraordinary reason, pictures of American Presidents around the walls. There were only two people in the pub. Me, on a stool at one end of the bar, and Oswald seated at the other end. Oswald was leafing through a pile of all the popular dailies, trying to work out how many times he had been scooped. It was, I suppose, about eleven o'clock in the morning.

Through the doors came a tall, military-looking man in an

Austin Reed overcoat, and a hat of the kind that is usually adorned with fishing flies. He looked around the bar. I noticed that, although the coat was once an expensive one, it was getting just slightly into the gravy-stain area, and that the hat, although worn with a certain style, had seen better days. The military-looking man strolled up to the bar, and stood in a position equidistant from me and Oswald. The landlord approached.

"Hullo there," said the military man.

"Good morning, sir!" said the landlord.

"I wondered," said the military man, as if he were not really interested in the answer, "if you could possibly do me a little cheque."

There was a horror-struck pause. Then the landlord said: "I'm afraid not, sir."

The military man smiled to himself and nodded. He was simply checking it out anyway, his smile seemed to say.

"Surely, surely," he said. And then, still with the same, tolerant, Christian smile on his face, he turned and strode to the exit. The landlord returned to his seat, shaking his head. Oswald looked at me and I looked at Oswald.

"There but for the Grace of God . . ." said Oswald. And after that we were friends.

It occurs to me that, over the last few years, if I had to draw up a balance sheet of activities, with headings like TALKING DRINKING SCREWING WRITING READING or even WORKING—the largest slice of time would be seen to have been taken up by the first two activities, and most of them indulged in the company of Oswald Garvey. We must have spent at least a year in a pub in Ladbroke Grove, challenging the locals to bar billiards and losing. It's a huge, cavernous Irish pub—mainly inhabited by junkies, dope-dealers and people who tried and failed to get jobs on the Alternative Press. Every six months, the brewery fly over some yokel from Sligo or Connemara. The yokel wipes up the joints, the vomit and the blood left by the customers, puts in a pile carpet and paints the whole place mauve or brown or whatever colour reminds him of home. For a few days, real people start to use the pub, men with big, red necks, Irish accents, dark suits,

153

heavy hands and jobs in Construction. Then, little by little, the scrubby denims and the joints and all the dead-eyed denizens of Ladbroke Grove crawl back in, until, at the end of a month, everything in the place is smashed, dirty and riddled with sexually transmitted diseases once again. Almost the only constant customers were Oswald and me—sitting in the saloon bar over our Guinness, warming ourselves at the fire of lost youth.

And, now I'm being honest about my parents and everyone I can think of, I might as well pay Oswald the same compliment. Face up to it, Steel, you're not as interesting as you'd like to be. You lied about Ellen manipulating you into marriage, tricking you into this house. You wanted it as much as she did, maybe more. You wanted, and want, a small semi with a Marina 1300 and 2.4 kids and a woman who'll cook and scrub and scrub and serve the first clean kiss when you return from work. And what do you want to do when you've got them? You want to sit up in the window like a cardboard cut-out, tapping out an unpublishable novel so that when your son (it'd *have* to be a son) returns from the last Direct Grant School left standing in the Western Hemisphere, looks up and sees you, he can beat his little fists on the garden fence and say "WHY DO I HATE MY DADDY?" But you haven't got the guts to admit this—so you work the poor woman into a novel and bitch about her behind her back because you feel guilty . . . (note to self—I do think the Ellen bits in the novel are rather good. Separation of artistic and private morality. Tremendous. What a brain!)

And, getting back to Oswald—you use Oswald as another form of alibi. You wish to remain young. In the absence of strange black powder or a suitable portrait to age in your stead, you get hold of a perfectly innocuous journalist and involve the poor lad in some ghastly re-run of the school dorm. I mean, face it Martin—you almost bought College scarves for you and Oswald. You fitted out a corner of your life, an ivy-covered segment, and tried to do that most shameful of things—prolong the irresponsibility of youth by artificial means. Such as pinball. If we've clocked up twelve months in the pub over the last few years, we must have wasted at least two years in pinball (which

154

leaves, in case you hadn't noticed, four years for travelling, screwing, reading, working and sleeping). I can still see Oswald surreptitiously tilting the machine in the Lots O' Fun, Charing Cross Road. For some strange reason he calls the machine "Jacko". One of my funniest memories is of him easing its little legs off the floor—and flushing with guilt when Jacko flashes TILT TILT TILT at him, angrily.

Oh fuck it. I love the guy. It's that simple. The way I love Mummy and Daddy and the cat next door and Harold Wilson and the whole wide world. I'm the Pollyanna of Brixton, playing the glad game all the way to the bank, a big-hearted C & W sentimentalist who loves everybody but does nothing about it. I will allow myself one more memory (why *memory*? Life has to go on even if you've stopped writing about it. I suppose it's true that the bits you've written about can never go on in quite the same way, but I don't think that authorship does anything more than reinforce the natural process of decay. It is true that I feel rather guilty writing this down. But it gives me pleasure. So I will.)

We were on holiday in a place called Orebic in Jugoslavia—a resort famous for its jellyfish and inaccessibility—Oswald, Ellen, me and a girlfriend of Oswald's called Thunderer. This wasn't her proper name but it was what everyone called her for some reason. Anyway—Oswald and I had gone swimming and Ellen and Thunderer were being bored to death by a local monk out of whom they hoped to screw some of the local hooch. We were on a beach about a mile from the village—a bare sweep of rock under a cliff, with the bay a terrific blue and, opposite, a tiny, pointless, deserted island. I forget what we'd been talking about but suddenly Oswald said:

"I knew a girl once..."

I knew better than to attempt a direct question. In order to get the anecdotal juices flowing I said, casually:

"Yeah?"

"And she *told* me," said Oswald, after a pause, "that she was thinking of committing suicide."

"Never!" I said, closing my eyes and feeling comfortable.

"She did," said Oswald, "and the weird thing was—I quite

155

liked her you know? . . . but it didn't worry me that much. Oh I mean it worried me. But not that much. Isn't that bad?"

"I don't know," I said.

"Well," said Oswald, sifting sand through his fingers, "there ought to be people around who you really miss. I mean people who are . . . essential. Don't you think?"

"Yeah," I said.

An awkward silence.

"There are some people like that," I said into the sand.

"I suppose so," said Oswald in a theoretical tone of voice. "I mean I suppose you represent in a way . . . that, I suppose . . ."

"Well certainly," I said, as if he had just scored a clever debating point, "well certainly I feel that about you. You know?"

"Sure sure," said Oswald.

By now we were both violently embarrassed.

"I'm going to face the jellyfish," he said, jumping to his feet and beating a tattoo on his chest. He can make his chest look rather impressive by breathing in and shifting his stomach a foot upwards in a vertical direction.

I watched him walk towards the water, pondering the English and our inability to let our feelings speak, the coldness that conceals so much love. How to get us to confess that half sexless affection we feel for each other? Because after all, time moves on, and, in a year, or two years, it may be too late, and we'll never have said the thing we should have to each other, and to the people we knew and loved as friends. Oswald struck out towards the island, bravely. I watched him until the sun hurt my eyes, then lay back on the beach. Even when you closed your eyes, I remember, the sun burned your lids, and there was a red mist, clamouring at you, making it difficult to think.

In a minute I'll get up and leave this paper and walk out on to the landing. Oswald will still be sitting on the stair. We'll have one more drink. I'll try not to patronise, misunderstand, write off, take for granted or otherwise abuse him. Maybe I'll try to say some of the unspoken things between us. And tomorrow I will see Ellen and try to act in the same way. It is only by constant thought, and constant attention that I will keep myself from sliding back into the mud. There will still be a novel. It will include both Ellen and Julie, but I am measuring it in my head against reality all the time, waiting for just the right moment to let it slip, to choose the time when I can unpack my heart, not with words only, like a mere drab, but with the still and lasting chords of a story.

And after the last drink it'll be bed. Good old bed.

PART THREE

19

Thursday 11.30 p.m.

The moment I woke this morning I knew something was up. I had the feeling immediately the light hit my eyes. It wasn't just that I felt that I'd been rinsing out my mouth with old ashtrays. That's fairly standard. It wasn't just that I had to go through the now familiar routine of expecting Ellen's face to loom up at me from under the duvet (which, by the way, I haven't changed for two weeks and is becoming vaguely greasy) or that the man next door was indulging in a veritable orgy of high decibel commercial radio. The technique for coping with this involves running headfirst at the wall, picking up one of Ellen's old shoes en route, and beating out an irregular rhythm at head height. This usually leads to him beating out a rhythm in reply until we have a cheerful, jungle-style conversation on the go.

But none of this was the problem. It was the fact that, although I could see it was ten thirty, the house was suspiciously quiet. And Oswald is a notoriously early riser. He could, of course, have overslept. But, much more likely, this *could* mean that he had woken up early, panicked about his indiscretion last night and departed in a hurry to inform Ellen that I might be on my way. For the moment, I had Oswald in the house, which meant that he was on my side—to let him slip back to Archway and the dreaded Jackie could lose me my current advantage. In a state of nervous dread, I selected a dressing-gown and set out for the front room where, as I recalled, Oswald had fallen asleep at about three a.m. in the middle of a discussion about News Value.

There were hopeful signs that Oswald was still around. There were four crumpled packets of Gold Leaf on the stairs and to the pile of rubbish in the hall had been added the traditional fragments of paper covered in what looks like cuneiform but is, in fact, shorthand. It was then, as a sharp, stabbing pain began behind my eyes, that I remembered that last night we had finished eight cans of Guinness, half a bottle of Southern Comfort and quantities of an obscure Jugoslav spirit, given to Oswald by a friendly tramp on a train from Barking to Charing Cross. I also had a vague recollection of Oswald wearing a large china bowl on his head and pacing around the kitchen reciting Yeats at top volume. I steadied myself on the banister and carried on down.

As I reached the hall, the phone went. I heard a scrabbling sound, then a crash and then Oswald, rattling out our number. It was impossible to tell from his voice whether he was asleep or awake. There was a pause and then he said:

"Oh. Hi. Ellen."

I froze. The conversation went on.

"Yeah yeah I did, I'm afraid. I *know*. No, I'm sorry but I thought it was . . . right. No he's fine, fine. I was a bit . . . pissed actually."

I stole, on tippytoes, round the corner of the room. Oswald was pacing to and fro, shrouded in the blanket I had given him last night. He looked very Roman.

"*No*, not at all no . . . I mean I . . . sure, *sure* I did and if you . . . well if you . . . sure I mean if you . . ."

He was so absorbed in throwing helpful emotional interjections down the line that he didn't see me until it was too late. I leaned over his shoulder, took the phone from him and said:

"Hullo Ellen it's me. Martin."

Oswald grinned nervously and backed away towards the bookcase, scratching his head. I got no answer. Would she put down the phone?

"How are you?"

Still no answer.

"Are you very . . . annoyed with me about something?"

No reply.

"Is that it?"

After a long pause:

"Maybe."

In a tight little voice, still with some humour in it but also with that note of frozen paranoia that Ellen sometimes gets on the phone. She sounded as if a gang of kidnappers were holding a shotgun to her head.

"Look, it's all got a bit stupid, love, hasn't it? A bit . . . er . . . out of control."

I had now started pacing as well. But both of us still kept our eyes on the floor. Oswald looked as if he too were telephoning an important message to someone.

"You see . . ." I went on, ". . . er . . . I mean I wasn't sure whether it was all a gag . . . know what I mean?"

"Yes I do."

Very small voice. Very precise.

"*Is* it a gag I mean . . . ?"

"Sort of. I mean it started . . ."

A deep breath from her.

"It started out that way."

"But now it's more serious."

"Er . . . I suppose thinking about things and . . . yes I suppose it is."

"Look Ellen I'd like to see you."

"Oh."

"Look we should. I mean if it is serious you know fine. If it is sort of . . . endsville, I mean we just ought to talk."

"I suppose so."

Something was seriously wrong with Oswald. He was now crouching by the net curtains, his blanket round his shoulders, Pocohontas style, peering into the mid-distance. He had seen something that worried him and, by the agitated little movements of his head, I could see he was about to tell me something. I ploughed on regardless with my heavy-handed attempt to Save My Marriage.

"Ellen, can I come and see you?"

"Martin—"

163

"Oswald gave me your address. I know you're with Jackie."
That shook her slightly. The balance of power altered.

"Look, love—" she started. But I didn't let her finish. Keep on
with the attack, pushing down the defences already developed in
a week away from me. Jesus how fragile our affairs are!

"Now you have to tell me, love, because I'm not stupid and I
have been doing a bit of thinking. Is it me and Julie?"

A pause. Out of the corner of my eye I saw Oswald hopping to
and fro like a man suddenly caught short many miles from a
public convenience. He was now waving his right hand up and
down. What had he seen? Martians perhaps. Let them come, I
thought, and got on with the business in hand. She still hadn't
answered.

"I saw her the other night. Really jokey."

"Yes?"

"Is it Julie and the ... er ..."

I became embarrassed about mentioning my novel in front of
Oswald. I could already hear the cracks. And she couldn't have
left me *just* because of the novel, but—

"Is it the novel thing?"

Long pause. Oswald's head jerked to attention.

"Partly. Partly."

"What else?"

"What it ... represented perhaps. It's very complicated. I
mean the thing is I suppose I'm frightened of hurting you
about—"

"Look I can get into me being a worm. I just want to *talk* about
this."

Oswald was now bouncing up and down like a gnome testing a
bed in a department store. In a flurry of panic. Completely
having forgotten my problem. I ignored him, pressing on, trying
to nail her in the last few seconds. She thought about it, wavered
and then said, in a cold and businesslike voice, a voice that held
out no hope of anything:

"O.K. But be here before twelve thirty. At one I've got to take
the kids up to Whitestone Pond."

"I'll be there."

164

The phone clicked at the other end and, as it did, I heard Oswald moaning softly. I turned to him and, just as I did, the doorbell rang, brash and sudden. I placed my ear closer to Oswald, who was now screwing his face up with the agony of it all, and heard him say:

"Mart. This is one for you, I fear."

"Uh?"

"The door. The *door*."

I was now feeling like an overloaded computer. Information was coming at me from too many sources. My head whirling, I went through to the hall and yanked back the front door. There in front of me, instead of a Martian, was Louise. Actually, I think I would have preferred a small green man with a ray gun and antennae. Louise is one of Oswald's current "problems". Oswald never has affairs these days, but "problems" with whom he is sleeping. Louise is very small with a shock of frizzy hair and tends to wear T-shirts and jeans. I noticed, with the terrible clarity of the possessed, that, on her left breast, was a large yellow sticker, on which was written the words "HAVE A NICE DAY!" I stared at this, rooted to the spot by its inanity, as she squeaked:

"Is Oswald there, please?"

"No," I said, sizing up the situation at a glance, "Oswald had to go to California."

"California!" she squeaked, "oh *really*!"

"Yes," I said, "really. Farewell, Louise, and have a nice day."

I was about to close the door on her, as she palpitated before me like a rabbit, when, sensing danger, she moved a little way into the hall, her little face alive with suspicion.

"Are you *sure* he's not here?" she piped, in the way I imagine a vole talking, if voles should ever take time off to speak about themselves.

"See for yourself!" I said, grandly, and, turning, I waved my hand at the empty hall and the still empty stairs, making sure that my feet blocked a more serious incursion into the territory. She looked. I smiled down. And, at that moment, from the front room, Oswald loped his way into the hall and down towards the kitchen, shoulders hunched and head down, ducking and weaving as he went like a man dodging machine-gun fire. What prompted this move I have not to this day discovered. Maybe he really was taken short.

The effect on Louise was electric. Letting out her highest and most agitated squeak so far ("Oswald...!") she ran past me, her chubby arms outstretched. As she went, I noticed that on her left buttock was another one of the yellow stickers. It said "SEE YA AROUND!" I decided to follow its advice. Oswald was perfectly capable of looking after himself. Anyway, I was already beginning to suspect him of having manoeuvred the whole situation. He can't bear not to be the centre of emotional attention and it was quite possible that he had deliberately invited Louise as a good potential diversion.

I bounded up the stairs, two at a time. Twelve thirty she had said. It was already nearly a quarter to twelve. I ran into the bedroom. Car keys? The bedroom. No. Spectacles. If I can find the spectacles I can find the car keys because I put the car keys next to the spectacles when I was in the television room. Television room. The car keys were in the television room. The spectacles weren't. That leaves bathroom or kitchen. I was now in Panic Overdrive. I could hear Oswald and Louise squealing at each other like a couple of hamsters, down below. I headed for the bathroom. Spectacles. Great.

Down the stairs, two at a time, I went. At the foot of the stairs I stopped. *Up* the stairs I went, two at a time, into the study, and picked up the manuscript of the novel all fifty thousand words of it, half-typed, half-handwritten on grubby cream wove pinched from my father's study over a period of several years. Then down the stairs again. At the bottom of the stairs, flushed with excitement, I turned. In the kitchen, Louise was pummelling Oswald's back as he cringed away in mock terror.

"Bash him, Louise!" I called. "Bash him as hard as you like. Knee him in the balls. Make him suffer. You do it!" They didn't hear me. I raced out into the street, slamming the door after me, the excitement of the chase now in my blood, singing in my ears. At half past twelve, just under an hour from now, I would at least be able to talk to Ellen, something I hadn't been able to do since this thing blew up. And that was half the battle. Maybe if I'd talked to her a bit more earlier, I wouldn't be going through all this. I looked wildly to right and left, saw my car and headed for it, like a fox on the run.

20

I say, glibly, my car. The vehicle is not actually mine. One of the advantages of my job, apart from the opportunity to meet and sneer at the famous (no man is a hero to a T.V. Researcher), is that I get a free supply of cars. The system works like this. I send a letter to a senior flunkey, explaining that I need a car to investigate some mythical politician in, shall we say, Leeds. They then phone up a hire car company, and, in due course, a woman dressed like an air hostess, jangling a fat bunch of keys, arrives at my office. "Your car, Mr Steel," she says, and I nod and smile and drive away.

Some three weeks later I telephone the office whence she came, in an executive frenzy, and say words to the effect of "Haven't you come to take away that car yet?" pretending that it has been waiting for them for weeks. Now, rule number one of large organisations is No One Knows What Anyone Else Is Doing. And rule two is—No One Gives A Fuck Anyway. If it's a public company—it's Government Money; if it's private—it probably all belongs to some dead American. Needless to say this rule does not apply to anyone earning less than four thousand a year. I earn just over that amount. And so, in due course, men from the Company arrive, stammering out apologies and drive the offending vehicle away to the "Depot" where immigrants throw spanners at it. Three days later I send another letter to another BBC flunkey, saying I wish to investigate an obscure M.P. in, shall we say, Scotland, and the process starts all over again.

There is only one drawback. The companies from whom I rent these cars, follow the basic Fraternal Hire Company Rules, which are:

No. 1.   Buy attractive uniforms for all staff.
No. 2.   Provide free folders containing Map of Britain and free Currency Exchange Guide—even if hirer is British.
No. 3.   Make sure all cars are a Heap of Old Tin.

With the result that, often, in the middle of the three-week loan period, the car gives a groan and collapses on me. When this happens, I simply phone up the firm, scream abuse at them, and men quaintly disguised as mechanics are sent out to me. I endeavour to explain the basic principles of the internal combustion engine to these said "mechanics" and, in a matter of hours, am back on the road. Simple.

All this is simply a prelude to explaining why it is, when I got, or rather leapt, into the car this morning, turned the key in the ignition and heard a high metallic cough, a dry orgasm of machinery from deep within the engine, I did not waste time opening the boot or bonnet, peering in, or in persuading some passer-by to push me some distance down the road. When a hire car croaks, it croaks. That ought to be their slogan. I, therefore, jumped out of the car and got on with the serious business of kicking its nearside wing and shouting at it. I was, as I think I explained, very late.

I was kicking and screaming at the vehicle when I heard a rap at the window. I turned, to discover Louise's face, pressed against the glass, a-goggle with worry and concern. She pointed to the car. I gave her the thumbs down signal. Still a-goggle with worry and concern, she left the window, obviously about to make helpful suggestions. That was more than I could stand. Giving the car a last, vicious kick just under the headlights, I put the keys in my jacket pocket and sprinted for the main road as hard as I could. After the hot weather of the last few days, today was curiously cool and a midsummer breeze cooled my face as, pacing myself, I crossed over, past the launderette, the chip shop and the pub and headed for Clapham North tube station.

My lungs were making a funny, sandpapery noise as I rounded the bend and got the station entrance in my sights. On the other side of the road two men in jeans were nailing up a sign that read "HALAL BUTCHER : CARIBBEAN STYLE". I came abreast of a greengrocers' shop with trays of fly-blown lettuces, sweet potatoes and watermelons out on the pavement. I ran out between two cars, dodged a bus and reached the booking hall. No time to get a ticket—I went straight through and down the escalator, my shoes beating a high speed rattle on the wooden slats of the stairs. Round the corner, *cut* through the archway, *turn* the bend, and—

And. There before me was the station platform, a thin strip of land, entirely surrounded by railway. Usually at about this time of day a peaceful sort of platform. The odd youth kicking a chocolate machine, an old lady, a malfunctioning indicator and that's about it. A kind of urban Adlestrop suspended in time—a place to stop and read the paper and wonder whether a train would come, and, if it did come, whether it would make any difference or solve anything.

Not, however, today. It looked like Saigon the day the Americans left. People were packed ten and twelve deep, so tight that they hadn't even any choice about which way they looked— the only thing they could move was their heads. There must have been nearly a thousand humans there. As I stood at the top of the stairs, hundreds of shifty little eyes rotated in my direction. They seemed to be saying "Don't join us. Please. Can't you see What Has Happened?" I started down the stairs and there, on a hastily erected blackboard at the end of the platform, read the reason for the trouble. Someone had scrawled in chalk:

"PASSENGERS WILL EXPERIENCE DELAYS TO ALL DESTINATIONS. THIS IS DUE TO A PERSON UNDER THE TRAIN AT STOCKWELL."

I thought about taking my place in this nucleus of a stampede, but decided against it. It would probably take them hours to unglue this unfortunate at Stockwell. I turned and, watched by the same tragic commuters' eyes, made my way back up to the surface. In the booking hall a large West Indian was leaning casually against the top of the escalator. He was wearing a bright check jacket, and dark glasses.

"Pretty bad down there?" he said.

"Hell," I said, "you wouldn't get this in Jamaica. Right?"

"I wouldn't know," said the man, "I never been to Jamaica."

Taking a deep breath I switched back into the running mode. My scheme was this—the quickest way of reaching Archway is by tube, so, in the absence of a taxi, I would be best off getting some other line than the Northern to within striking distance of the place and then administering the *coup de grâce* with a bus. Bus travel in London is not for long distances. It is a wonderful way of meeting people, of picking up scraps of local knowledge, but as a way of getting from A to B it is a total non-starter. I moved off up the high road towards Stockwell, a station served by both the Northern and the Victoria Lines; I might even pick up a bus on the way.

To cope with this possibility, I evolved a method of progress known as the hop-skip-and-look technique. This consists of a brisk movement, followed by a jerk over the right shoulder to check that one is not being trailed by a large double-decker. It can also be run in tandem with Backward Running, which is effective, although it can be dangerous, especially at unexpected road junctions. I was about a hundred yards up from Clapham North station, when I saw, in one of my backward running sessions, nothing other than a bus with "STOCKWELL" written on the front. The stop was too far away, but I did a quick calculation and estimated that it would have to stop at the lights, some twenty or thirty yards down the road; I ran; the bus overtook me, and then (thanks be to God) the lights changed to red and the bus squealed to a halt.

It was not until I got up to the vehicle that I realised that it was one of those one-driver efforts. Impossible to leap lightly onto the platform, under the admiring eyes of young female passengers. I ran up to the front of the bus, and, peering through the door, electrically operated from within, tried to attract the driver's attention. He was a red-faced, sleepy-looking man, staring ahead of him morosely, waiting for the lights to change. I tapped on the glass. Very slowly, he turned towards me, like a fish in an aquarium, baffled by the outside world.

"The door," I mouthed, "—could you open the door?" His

171

eyes narrowed. Inside the bus, life, I felt, was very different; he and I were living on different time scales. Making a last, frantic effort, I pointed at myself and then at the bus, nodding and smiling. The driver did not un-narrow his eyes. A shadow passed across them—a distant memory of some other place, some other time, where, possibly, all this had happened before. Then—he engaged gear and the bus roared off up the road. As it passed, forty or so passengers stared out at me, all very like fish, like contented, looked-after fish on their way to a larger and better equipped tank.

It was back to running after that—running and a long, complicated curse on London Transport. The curse goes (should anyone wish to use it, it isn't copyright) "When did you last seeabloodyfucking politician on a bleeding BUS orableeding TRAIN come to that and now that Ithinkofitwhen-didyouseeanyoneinchargeofbleedinglondontransport *on*ableed-ing BUS orcometothinkofitonableedingbastardsodding TRAIN." And so on. Somehow I reached Stockwell without vomiting blood, limped into the entrance, and there in front of me was the friendly blackboard bearing the inscription:

"BECAUSE OF PEOPLE ON THE LINE PASSENGERS WILL EXPERI-ENCE DELAYS TO ALL DESTINATIONS."

Undeterred, I approached the booking office and pressed my face to the plastic grille. I noticed a policeman over by the escalator, shepherding people out of the place.

"Er—"

Before I had a chance to speak, the booking clerk said:

"You'll have a long wait."

"No," I said, "it's the Victoria Line I want."

"Right," he said, "there's a person under a train."

"I *know*," I said patiently, "but they're under a Northern Line train. Right?"

"No, mate," he replied, "there's one under a Northern Line train and another under a Victoria Line train."

"What is it?" I said, "a train spotters' suicide pact?"

"Don't be so bleeding callous," said the booking clerk.

Hectic with fury, I turned away and strode out into the street.

A fat lady approached me, a shopping basket on her arm.

"What's up?" she said, indicating the policeman.

"There are two people under two different trains," I said crisply.

"Oh *no*," she said.

"Oh yes," I said, "and, frankly, I tell you this. I pray to the Lord God above that both of them are London Transport employees."

She stared after me, aghast. As I crossed the roundabout by Stockwell I caught sight of a clock outside a shop. It was twelve fifteen. The Tatler Cinema was showing *Midnite Plowboy* and *When Girls Undress*. I seriously thought about giving up and going in, but, loyal to the last, good old Steel ploughed up towards Kennington, the only hope left to him a taxi, a good old London black cab.

21

As I walked, I thought about the delicate balance that there exists between me and Ellen. If Oswald had stayed on with her a few more days, she could well have left me for good; her attitudes would have hardened. If Oswald hadn't been so even handed with us, she wouldn't have phoned me this morning. I was pretty sure it was only the nagging worry that Oswald and I might be having a good time that had made her phone. Despite his worries about being a Go-Between Oswald is, in fact, perfect for the job. By being impartially fair to both of us, he serves to intensify our games but never increases or minimises the risks involved. After that, I thought again about how to convince her that I had changed. Would that produce a different kind of honesty in her? Would she believe me? You can convince someone you're going to be a better and nicer person only by *being* a better and nicer person. And in order for them to see how you've changed they have to have the confidence to live with you or at least to see you for some period of time. How was I going to prove anything to her, when all my attempts at being a reasonable human being have, to date, ended in cattiness or paranoia? I hugged the novel closer to me.

In the middle of the road came a taxi, indicator yellow and welcome. I raised one arm, trying to look rich, generous and anxious to go wherever the taxi-driver wanted instead of pursuing some selfish plan of my own. The last occasion on which I boarded a taxi, the driver told me he was "going home" and could only take me to Fulham. I explained I didn't want to go to Fulham. I was by this time sitting in the back of the cab. "Listen," said the taxi-driver, "I'm going to Fulham. You can come if you like. If you don't like—hop out." In the end he agreed to take me somewhere where he thought I might get another cab. We reached Shepherd's Bush. Not a cab in sight. He peered around hopefully and said, pointing to an old Wolseley abandoned on the Hammersmith Road, "There's one!" "That," I said, "is a private car." He relapsed into silence, and hunched up over the wheel, potato-faced with sorrow at the situation. "This has become a battle of wills, hasn't it?" I said. "Yes," he said, sadly. After a half-hour wait he took me to Paddington, and left me at the taxi rank, by which time an uneasy mutual respect had developed between us. Taxi travel is, after all, not a game for softies.

So I put my whole soul into the hailing gesture, and as the taxi swerved into the side of the road, I stepped out, extended a seigniorial hand towards the cab-door and put sweetness, firmness and money into the way I said:

"Archway please."

Greatly to my surprise, the man nodded and allowed me in. An eccentric obviously. Leaning back in my seat I ran through my opening speech to Ellen.

When we reached the centre of town—it was already twelve forty. I'd almost forgotten the schedule in my glee at having procured a taxi. This might mean that she wouldn't speak to me. Once again I thought about going back and jacking the whole thing in, and, once again, came down on the side of trying. I decided to go straight to Whitstone Pond, and, with the feeling of relief that accompanies postponement of a deadline, engaged the driver in a long conversation about V.A.T. that I hoped he found as boring as I did. The wind had now become quite strong, blowing through the trees in Regent's Park, scattering paper on the pavement outside Lord's and raging round that improbable palm tree at St John's Wood station. The meter ticked. We stopped at innumerable lights. I noted, idly, the makes of different cars. And so we arrived at Hampstead Village and turned up the narrow, boutique-ridden hill that leads up to the Heath. I was in the wrong place, and three-quarters of an hour late. I had had no indication on the phone that Ellen even wanted to see me, except perhaps as a means of reasserting her claims to Oswald's friendship. But, as I handed over two pound notes and the taxi-driver did an unconvincing impression of a man looking for change, I felt sure that things were going to be all right. I had to convince her I had changed. By words. I'm good at that. And, just in case, I had a gesture up my sleeve as well. A gesture I imagined would cost me nothing. Just shows how wrong you can be.

They weren't by the side of the pond. There was a man in waders pursuing a large toy launch and that was about all. I went over to the pavement on the south side, looking over towards London, and, at the bottom of the steep, clay hill that slopes away from the road, I saw them. A tall, red-headed girl, surrounded by ten or fifteen children, primary-school age, all in blue anoraks. Some of the children were towing what looked like a polythene bag along the grass. Others were gathered round her, her hair falling across her face as she talked to them. My face suddenly felt flushed. I saw her put out her hand to one of them: then she looked up, laughing. Blinking rapidly, I stepped down on to the path and made my way towards them. I counted up the days I hadn't seen her—eight, ten was it? One of the children had fallen over and Ellen was picking him up, dusting him down. I wondered why we hadn't had children. Me, I supposed. But *why* though? Scared? Too late for wondering about things like that. Oh sweet Jesus give me the strength and the ability to talk in coherent, continuous sentences!

She saw me when I was about twenty yards away. She didn't show any surprise. She straightened up and pushed back the hair from her eyes. She nodded, but she didn't smile. I felt she looked tired. The kids who had been playing with the polythene bag gave up and turned their attention to this new and interesting stranger. Ellen was holding a little Indian girl by the hand. The girl was wearing a blue anorak, a skirt and jeans under the skirt. She must have been about six or seven. I stopped about five yards away, at a loss for words. Then Ellen said:

"This is Gita."

"Hullo Gita," I said.

"Hullo!" said Gita.

A fat child who still trailed the string attached to the polythene bag stumped a little way in my direction. He looked up, accusingly.

"Are you her boyfriend?" he asked.

And, before I had time to answer satisfactorily, he turned to Ellen and said:

"Miss—is he your boyfriend?"

"No," said Ellen, without the trace of a smile, "he only admires me from afar."

None of them got this. I wasn't sure I did. Mainly to try and break an uncomfortable feeling that I was fixed to the surface of the Heath by nine-inch nails, I strolled over to the polythene bag, rather too casually. I nodded down at it and turned back to Ellen and the circle of tiny black, white and brown faces, and said:

"What's this then?"

"Oh," said Ellen, "it's the Form Kite."

"Ah," I said.

"We were trying to fly it."

"Only," said a very small girl in a brushed nylon coat, "John Jo broke it."

"I didn't," said another child.

"*Oh* yes you did," said the girl, looking how I imagined her mother looked when the old man came back pissed. There was a pause. It seemed like there was just me and Ellen and these kids, painted on to the blowy landscape of the Heath, like Lowry figures. Then, at last, Ellen moved; she turned to the kids and said:

"Martin and I are going to have a chat. Now why doesn't everyone get on with flying the kite."

The kids were not at all keen on this idea. Something funny was going on and they were going to find out what it was. They stood around, silent, like aliens unable to find their way back to the ship, as Ellen, with great difficulty, disengaged her hand from Gita's.

"It's nice to see you," I couldn't stop myself saying, as she came towards me.

"Miss—" said the girl in the brushed nylon coat, "Miss it's broken Miss."

"In that case," said Ellen firmly and maternally, "you can all get on with mending it, can't you?"

It was in the balance for a couple of seconds. Either they were going to sway forward like the Roman Mob, badly in need of bread and circuses, or they were going to follow orders. Then, greatly to my relief, the fat child started to pull the thing towards him, chanting "I'm doing the ki-ite, I'm doing the ki-ite", the communal will trembled and broke into a thousand pieces as child after child swarmed round the new centre of attention, leaving only Gita staring forlornly out of the group, gazing after Ellen with the unsatisfied eyes of unrequited love.

We walked up the hill a little, to where we could sit and watch them. I said:

"You're really good with those kids."

"Yes?"

"Yes."

"Just my job."

It was funny, I thought to myself, how I had always taken her job for granted. It might have been a good thing to say, but I'd already gone far enough. Gita watched us from a distance, and then, when she'd abandoned all hope, walked slowly and unenthusiastically to the group round the kite. She stood at the edge, rubbing her eyes with her knuckles.

"And now," I said, "I suppose we talk about Me and You."

"Yes," said Ellen, "I suppose we do."

22

At the back of the wind had come, even more unexpected, rain. Not as much as a shower, just the occasional drop, stinging the face. I put my hands up to my face, and, taking care not to look at her, began operations. Over by the Vale of Health, about the only other person to be left out, a big lady in a caramel coat, walked a labrador home to tea.

"It was really your reading ... *the* novel, wasn't it?"

"Like I said ... partly."

"Yeah ... but for that amazing coincidence..."

"About Julie you mean?"

"Mmm."

"Oh it isn't a coincidence that I know Julie," said Ellen. "We all know each other in this racket."

"What racket's that?"

"The graduate racket. The middle-class racket I suppose."

"Ah."

She looked abstracted. But at least she was talking.

"The thing is," she continued, "it's a very odd feeling. To pick up a book by someone you know and to recognise someone. It was really weird—like seeing her at a station and thinking *can* that be her? No—it can't be."

I couldn't help being flattered by the fact that we were discussing my novel at such length. Trying to keep the smirk off my face, I said:

"And you were shocked?"

"Er ... a bit. In a way. I thought—Jesus this *is* Julie—must be. I don't know why—I just knew. Funnily enough, ever since she told me she'd been going out with a man who was ... writing her nasty letters, I had an obsession it was you, or rather *could* be you."

"And you thought the book was Nasty."

"Yes I did. I thought it was horrid. I thought it was a bit sick actually. A bit . . . paranoid. Not that that worried me. I'm not naïve enough to suppose that people's fiction gives any clue to their personality at all."

I swallowed. Jesus, the bitch was bright, I thought. And also, attractive. Maybe I wasn't being aggressive enough. It was quite simple really. Ellen had picked up a book of mine, read an unflattering portrait of a person who happened to be, by some fiendish, but not unsurprising, coincidence, a friend of hers. She had also realised that Yours Truly was Shit From Past of said friend. That was the issue—and here we were discussing literature!

"Look," I said, "I know you're pissed off about me and Julie and me not telling you about what I did to Julie and about me being a bit of a sod sometimes, I mean vindictive in a way, and—

"I'm not," said Ellen, cracking her fingers, "the funny thing is I'm not really pissed off about any of that. People tell lies—small lies really. There's a lot you don't know about me—meannesses, weaknesses. You expect to find those if you dip into someone's diary or someone's novel. They don't signify. What signifies is what you are at the moment."

"I suppose so."

I looked across at the class outing, still grouped around the kite. The fat child seemed to have made some technical breakthrough, because he was placing the machine reverently on the grass while another kid measured out a length of twine. I wondered why I was getting off so lightly. Ellen was speaking again.

"I'm not talking about your faults," she went on, "I know your faults. You're very bitter about some things, you're a coward, you lie sometimes. That doesn't make any difference to my loving you. If loving is worth anything at all, it's being able to deal with things like that. No. What happened between me and you was that I started to play a sort of game."

180

I swallowed hard again and listened. I didn't like that use of the past tense. Looking at her jacket draped over her shoulders and at that serious, caring face, I realised just how much I was scared of losing her. I didn't say any of this, but repeated, like a dull examinee:

"What sort of game?"

"Well. You see—writing is a sort of one-upmanship on people really. I used to write. Never told you about it. But I stopped because I found it was making me superior. Writing about people, watching them, kills a lot of things. It kills spontaneity, it kills, sometimes, the joy of sex, it kills life—eats it bit by bit. I don't think there's anything remarkable about that. In fact I think it's a commonplace."

"It needn't do those things."

"Let me finish anyway. So I started to play my games. My games don't go on paper. They were all between us. I was giving you things all the time, keeping one step ahead of you, playing you, adjusting you, as if you were a character in *my* book. And what's odd about that isn't that I was doing it—it's that I was doing it so desperately, so near to the edge. That the jokes could get so sour—and a two-day parting turn into a lifetime's separation. Are you listening?"

"I'm listening."

"Now don't get me wrong. I don't object to your writing at all. In fact it suits me very well. I have a life of my own to get on with. I don't want someone round my neck all the time. For instance, you may or may not have noticed that I have been a member of an organisation called the Labour Party and now I'm thinking of moving on. I am also involved in something known as the Women's Movement—"

"Ellen—"

"But when we talk about politics, how often does the conversation start and finish with your opinions about what you read in the newspaper this morning. When I've been to a meeting you don't want to know about it. For you my political work is the equivalent of a Victorian lady's stint at the soup kitchen. Isn't it?"

"Maybe. Maybe so. I mean we just never *talked* about these things."

It came back to the same problem. You remembered what you wanted to remember about people and forgot what didn't suit. When *had* she joined the Labour Party anyway and where was she moving on to?

"But *why* didn't we? Actually about a lot of it we did but you never bloody noticed. And why does it always have to be me making the running?"

"Because I'm—"

"When's my birthday?"

"Er—"

"Go on. When's my birthday?"

"28th July?"

"29th. What do I think about inflation?"

"Well—you think inflation is—"

I goggled.

"*I* don't know what you think about inflation."

"Well you bloody well should."

"Er—"

"But the point I'm trying to make is that I can cope with all of that. It worries me, sure, and if it gets too bad I'll be off like a shot. But the more unsavoury side of your character is not what concerns me now. Sure that was part of the reason for my getting out—the feeling that I could only get through to you by means of some spectacular gesture. But all that was containable—if you understand me."

"Not quite."

"It wasn't that bad. I can live with you having the emotional energy of a mollusc. That doesn't ultimately bother me. I happen to be in love with you, O.K?"

"Fine. Fine," I said, feeling chastened. If that was the case what were we arguing about?

"*But* although all this was going on, it was reading that novel that tipped me over the edge. Reading that novel was a bloody revelation to me. Not because of what it told me about you as an individual. But because it endangered my respect for you."

182

"Because it was so cynical and—"

"NO! For God's sake will you listen?"

She seemed tired and exasperated. I was tired and exasperated. Unbidden, my mind wandered off to other things. With an effort I switched it back on to the rails. Maybe we had had this conversation before only I hadn't been listening. Only now I had to listen. It was important.

"Because O.K. you're not the easiest person in the world to live with. But previously I've operated on the principle that there was some point to it all. I've never really thought about what you did up in that study. Treated it as a hobby I suppose, like Gardening. But on this occasion—with the Julie novel—maybe because I recognised her and that got me interested, I really sat down and read it. Read it carefully. I've never done that with anything of yours before."

Somehow this struck me as absolutely appalling. I had to admit, however, that it could be regarded as a just revenge for my not listening to anything she said. What was really frightening me was that she seemed to be leading up to something and I didn't know what it was. Some unexpected complaint that I would have to deal with impromptu. Playing for time, and wondering whether this was the longest serious conversation we had ever had about my Art and her Personality, I said:

"How do you mean?"

She treated this with the contempt it deserved.

"When I read that book, Martin, something snapped, and can I just say again for the millionth time that it *wasn't* because of you and Julie. It was because I thought it was a bloody awful book."

I felt a sick feeling in the pit of the stomach. This was what I had been trying to avoid all the way along the line.

"And you see that throws the whole calculation, doesn't it? It means that I can't respect you. You might as well be going off to the Territorial Army every morning. And that's pathetic, isn't it, Martin?"

"Look. I think it has—"

"You think it's good?"

"I don't know. I—"

183

"Because it isn't. It's bloody boring for a start."

"I thought the bit where the girl goes to the airport was—"

"Overdone."

Of course. It was perfectly clear. She was right. It was overdone. Help help help. She was still talking.

"You see, artists are supposed to get something back for all the pain and agony and peering at people through keyholes. But what did you get back? You got a heap of old rubbish back that's what. You sit up there waiting for your muse, but when she arrives she hands you a sub-standard episode of *Z Cars* or a dreadful, sterile re-creation of familiar faces in unfamiliar places. It's not the malice I mind, or even Julie. It's the fact of seeing malice or Julie so limply displayed. The only thing that matters as far as I'm concerned is doing good things. And don't run away with the idea that your book was bad because you were a nasty person. It's much easier to correct your morals than to correct your style. Get this into your head—the only two people in the world who even take time off to *think* about your style are me and you. The police can look after your morals and your mother and your father and a whole load of people."

"Look—"

"I'll finish what I have to say. So. After Oswald and I lit out, partly as a joke really, I went to a friend in Barnet and now I'm with Jackie and I'm asking myself, well *can* I spend the rest of my life tied to a man whom I love but don't respect?"

"Yes. Yes. I mean . . . I see really . . ."

It was obvious to me now, why hadn't it been obvious before? The real issue was the novel and the novel's merits. I'd been using anything I could to evade that. Almost in physical pain, I said to her:

"Er . . . don't you think that there's any . . . er . . . hope for it. . .?"

"For what?"

"The novel."

She looked at me full in the face for the first time for some minutes. I thought I read contempt in her expression. I wondered whether I should have asked a question to do with Life and not Art, at that juncture. It was too late now. With the angry impartiality of a good critic she said:

"Not really. I don't think you'll ever be a writer until you learn to tell the difference between fact and fiction. And I don't mean lying about things in real life. I mean the manipulation of experience to make a whole, to make something that lives, that gets up and walks away on its own. A Work of Art in her words. You're very clever and you can be very funny, but you're also very lazy. You don't use your bloody eyes. Or, when you do use your eyes, you don't use them in the right way. You seem to feel the need to hang a 'plot' or an apology for a story over the truth, to cover your tracks. You may even be *aware* of this but it doesn't stop you doing it. The frustrating thing is *I* can see what to do about it and I'm just jolly old Ellen who provides jokes and tea and a screw (occasionally) and Talks About Your Work. I'm not even allowed to have babies because of your bloody work."

"I—"

"And some of my intelligence (which is not inconsiderable) and my valuable time and energy is going into fuelling a book that isn't worth the paper it's written on. Sorry, Martin. Amanuensis to a Great Man's a bit of a sticky one, but Amanuensis to a Mediocrity—sorry no deal."

As if to provide a cheap metaphor for my literary endeavours, the infants were now trying, unsuccessfully, to get the Form Kite off the ground. The fat child was supervising two small black children. They held the ropy polythene structure aloft, while he and another infant ran forward, holding the string. On the word of command from the fat child, the two small black children let go of the kite. Which promptly fell to the ground. This then stimulated more Maintenance Work. The other children stood around watching open-mouthed. I took the manuscript of the novel out of my coat.

"Oh Jesus," said Ellen, "he's only brought it with him!"

It was at that moment I knew it was going to be all right, and, although it may not, on the surface, seem like much of a landmark, it is from that moment I date my new self. As big a shake-up for me, on the aesthetic front, as Proust and his

185

madeleine, a weird, tingling feeling as if a mild electric shock had been applied to the pleasure centres of my frontal lobes. Was it something about the way she said it? Or the way the Heath looked? Or those kids in the background? Anyway, it had Gestalt written all over it in big, black letters. It was the moment when I decided to make, not the gesture I had originally planned, but something more spectacular, and well, not more honest, but more *apparently* honest. More honest then, I hear the ghost of some long-dead philosopher mutter.

I had intended to give Ellen the manuscript and say to her, as solemnly as possible, "Here it is. Here's the offending article. I'm sorry I'm a shit. If you think it's too bitter and cynical and twisted—burn it. I won't mind." This was a fairly foolproof gesture, assuming that Ellen's beef against me was that I was cynical and twisted and spent too much time on work of national literary importance. If her beef was that not only was I cynical and twisted but also a bloody awful novelist, the gesture became less foolproof. Like all the gestures in all of my life, until that moment on the Heath this afternoon, I assumed that I was, if not a Great Novelist, at least a reasonable one. On receipt of her brief and succinct critique of the work, however, it was reasonable to assume that if I gave it to her, she might actually burn it.

I peeled off the top page. Two hundred odd neatly typed words. Quotation marks, adjectives, fictional people talking to each other, future Bovarys or Myshkins, in the form of Stephen Jarrett, Mary or whoever else . . . people who had not yet become real, love scenes, set up comedy scenes, bits of both our lives. I held up the paper and the wind whipped through it. Ellen was watching me now, for the first time with real attention. I stood up. She made as if to touch my arm, but, before she had abandoned the movement, I had let go of the paper and the wind had taken it.

She made no further move to try and stop me. I dealt off more and more pieces of paper and gave them to the wind, and the wind, suddenly strong, took them, and whirled them up against each other and the sky like a flock of birds; more and more paper I gave to the wind, and there were more and more patterns, now

186

scrappy, now arabesque, lifted up for everyone to watch, frozen in motion like confetti as the wedding camera snaps it, higher and higher in circles and stairways of paper, an arbitrary code, changing with each new gust of wind, until the whole novel, all fifty thousand words of it, representing at least two quids' worth of Steel Senior's stationery, and nearly ten years' worth of experience, was whirling and dancing its way towards the Vale of Health and the unsuspecting trees beyond.

And, in the same wind, the fat child's patience was rewarded. For what seemed like the twentieth time, he and his companions ran forward. For what seemed like the twentieth time his tiny, black sidekicks let go of the kite, and yet, on this occasion, for no good reason apart, possibly, from symmetry, the wind took the polythene and the struts, and the fat child, shortening the line gleefully, watched it climb higher and higher into the sky, up, up to the end of the rope—a miracle. And the pages of my sixteenth unpublished novel brushed against it on their way.

"Litter lout!" said Ellen. But she smiled, for the first time in ages.

23

What else we discussed this afternoon need not be gone into here. How it was an extraordinary coincidence her knowing Julie. How she'd always known how many lies I told about my past life (especially my past affairs). How it was, she said, transparently obvious that I'd only ever been with one other woman, but how that made her (she said) love me more. And I talked about how frightened I was of getting hurt by her, which was why I had lied and hidden in imaginary work and found it difficult, sometimes, to touch and kiss her as I should. It was a breaking of barriers, the collapse of hundreds of rigid habits and jokes that we'd built up over six years, and, as we talked, the kids did weirder and weirder things with the Form Kite, even Gita, at last, joining in and running and squealing with the others.

Oh we discussed Julie, and said how, really, it was simply that we had been too young for each other but of course she was a sweet person and we discussed Derek too, and Ellen told me how jokey it was phoning up Julie, getting both of us invited to dinner and then disappearing at the last moment. She told me about practical jokes she'd played when she was at school, sticking twigs up the trouser-legs of small boys, and how, at the age of six, she had forced her younger brother to dress up as the Emperor of Siam, sitting him on an upturned bucket, and prancing round him, singing his praises. She told me about a man she'd slept with when she was seventeen, in a camping site near Stratford-upon-Avon, who had leaned over and said afterwards: "I knew your body would accrue to me." We decided to have children, wondered whether they'd look like us and what we could do about it. We agreed that love was a matter of using your common sense. We were cunning, skilful with each other and, after twenty minutes' talk, I kissed her the way I hadn't done for a long time. I don't know why but there was something sad about us as well—two people huddling together because they knew the score so well.

The kids finally managed to smash the kite into tiny pieces and the fat child and two of his henchpersons jumped up and down on it for good measure. Fights started to break out. Somebody fell over. A girl got tangled up in the string. And, in the end, Gita stumped her way over to us and asked if they could go home. We took them up the hill, across to Hampstead Lane, somehow or other herding them on to a bus—change at Highgate Village and then down the hill to the grim houses and their parents. Ellen and I stood in the bus, now totally accepted as parent substitutes, arm in arm, kissing from time to time. The kids were no longer interested in us. They stared fiercely out of the windows at the passers-by, drawn into themselves against the rain, which was now coming in across the city harder and harder, in level fields of grey. They stared into the shops, bright with consumer durables. We took them to what Ellen called the "de-briefing centre", where they handed in their sandwich cartons, and Ellen gave them information about the next rendezvous. Then school broke up for the day. Suddenly there were lollipop men everywhere and Ellen and I were back to being normal adults.

What happened on the journey back? There was a tube and another bus and the rain continued and a woman said "That's summer over." And we discussed Oswald. Ellen told me how frantic he'd been when they got to Archway. We discussed Jackie in the light of my castration complex, and Ellen told me that she, Jackie, thought I was a Good Thing Basically. We resolved to go and have a meal when we got back. We couldn't stop touching each other or looking at each other. At Camden Town a very fat man with a very small dog got on and that set us giggling. Anything else? Not really.

When we reached the house, Oswald and Louise were in the front room. Oswald was teaching Louise the rules of chess. She was having some difficulty in remembering the names of the pieces. I noticed, with pleasure, that the yellow sticker reading "HAVE A NICE DAY" was no longer on her left breast, but over her right shoulder-blade, from which I deduced that, in my absence, intercourse, or at least heavy petting, had taken place. I found the idea cheering. They certainly looked effectively detumesced—with Oswald guiding her hands across the board, and, occasionally, stroking her wrist.

After a while (Louise having tried to move a rook diagonally for the third time in succession) the game disintegrated, and Louise engaged Ellen in what topics she thought would interest her, i.e. babies, clothes and cooking. Ellen's eyes glazed over and her mouth got to look like a steel trap. Oswald and I thrashed out the relationship of Trotsky to Lenin, in the light of the work of Isaac Deutscher. From time to time, Ellen threw me an anxious glance. When I heard Louise getting on to her sister's miscarriage, I suggested we went out for a drink. We went. In the pub, Ellen, Oswald and I discussed the relationship between the Trades Union Movement and the Women's Struggle, while Louise sipped nervously at a dry white wine (only, she informed us, 75 calories in Her Chart). After the pub, an Italian meal somewhere in the wilds of Clapham. Things were getting back to normal.

The Italian restaurant was laid out like a side-chapel in the shrine of Our Lady of Lourdes—there were fountains everywhere and, in the corner, a large colour blow-up of Lake Como had been pasted on to the wall. Not content with this, the management had stuck a mock-up of a window frame on top of it—perhaps to remind themselves of home. Oswald ordered cannelloni followed by lasagna as he said he was "on a pasta trip". Louise just managed to keep down some grilled trout, *no* potatoes please, and I consumed well over a litre of something called Carafino la Favorita. Then we had the final news of the day. I noticed that Oswald and Louise were unable to keep their hands off each other and had put this down to simple lust, but at the coffee stage, when Oswald had started trying to lick Louise's ear, Ellen said:

"What's up with you two?"

Oswald looked shifty. Louise beamed.

"You tell them," she said.

Oswald pulled at his chin.

"No. You," he said.

"Well," said Louise, "we had a talk this afternoon—"

"It's untrue!" said Oswald.

"*And*," went on Louise, "we came to a decision."

"Never!" said Oswald.

"We're going to get somewhere," said Louise. Oswald shook himself like a dog.

"I cannot deny the rumour entirely," he said.

"A flat!" said Louise, and added, in case we hadn't understood, "*together*!"

Ellen and I looked at each other. I wasn't quite sure what I felt. A bit like a parent whose eldest son tells him he's just got an Open Scholarship to Cambridge? A bit like a girl whose boyfriend tells her he has to go off and study these Indians in Venezuela—he'll be about ten years and can she wait? I don't know how I felt quite, but I knew that I was coming to the end of a phase in my life—not the School Phase, or the Wanking Phase or the Bachelor Phase, but the phase of being in a house with Ellen and Oswald and writing my journal and trying to make sense of things. I felt sad—the way you do at the end of a Phase, but, perhaps more than that, a deep sense of wonder and respect for Louise. How she'd managed to get Oswald to commit himself, with the help of only a calorie chart and a pair of lively little breasts, was beyond me. Had she used force? I looked at them both looking at me— sheepishly—and, feeling pretty sheepish myself, said:

"I hope you'll be very happy."

"A happy ending to all our troubles!" said Oswald.

"God Bless Us Every One!"

"God Bless Us!" said Ellen.

A waiter arrived at our table and handed us a menu in the shape of a fish:

"Someone's a-get married?" he asked, beaming in the manner of Italian waiters.

"All of us," said Oswald, "we're all getting married to each other."

"Is good at first," said the waiter, "after that—not so good."

To follow his two portions of pasta, Oswald ordered a double portion of profiteroles, a brandy, a coffee and another litre of Carafino which he described as Carafino Fantastico. I sat back in my chair, my head spinning, and tried to remember whether Ellen and I were married and, if we were, whether it would be possible to go through the whole thing again. The lights of the restaurant, the atmosphere of linen, and smiles being exchanged for hard cash, rocketed around in my brain, until the last brandy had been downed, the last profiterole swallowed, and we were groping our way towards Oswald's car. The waiter followed us to the door and stood, waving, happy to be in on the end of yet another unintelligible celebration. Clapham Common looked dark and bleak as we drove back, and Ellen and I sat very close. It occurred to me, as we swung round the lights at Clapham Common station, that, in the near future, it might be amusing for Ellen and me to visit Derek and Julie. Why not? We could make a reasonable foursome.

Oswald stamped wildly on the accelerator and hurtled the car in the direction of a tobacconist's window. Then, relenting, and deciding to live after all, he jerked the wheel to the right and we were safe in Acre Lane, under the yellow sodium lamps, with the wide pavements strewn with chip papers, fag packets and the flora of the concrete desert of South London. Ellen suddenly slackened her hold on my hand and turned to me. Her face was serious and pale:

"I meant what I said today," she said gently, "you know that don't you, love?"

"Abso*lutely*," I said, without paying very close attention.

"You've got to stop wasting your time like that. Or I'll leave you. And it'll be for good this time."

"Sure, love. Sure. I know that."

A pause. I didn't speak. What was I thinking about then? I don't remember exactly.

"I'm glad, love. Because I don't *want* to leave you."

Her hand tightened, and mine too in reply to hers.

I can hear the house, humming with typical activity as I write. Ellen is playing the B minor Mass, Oswald and Louise are having a row, and I'm here in my study, the Anglepoise lamp (bought by Ellen to go with the cork-tipped noticeboard) flooding the page with yellow light. I came up here an hour or so ago. Soon there'll be a crash from downstairs and Ellen will thump up the stairs; then, Oswald and Louise—the crash of the bedroom door, called goodnights and then total silence. I'll still be working here when they've all gone to bed.

You see, when we got back from the Italian meal, I went to the desk, unlocked the bottom right-hand drawer and took out the pages of this journal. Ellen doesn't know about that. She never will know about it. And if she knew I was looking at it now I'd be in trouble. But I can't tear myself away from it or from what it represents. Not yet. Not just yet anyway. I get physical pleasure just from touching it. Around fifty or sixty thousand words—all that's left of my aborted, sixteenth novel. I flicked through the pages and thought hard about all Ellen had said. The only thing that matters is the quality of the work. And, curiously enough, as I read what I'd written about myself, from day to day, it was like reading about someone else, like reading about a character in a novel. The characters, obstinately, live—and they're not quite Oswald or Ellen or Julie or Louise, but people in their own right, arguing and talking and screwing in their own way, irrespective of their originals. Strange.

The thing's written out in a couple of Ellen's old notebooks from school, in crabbed longhand. There are hardly any crossings out or revisions the way there are (or were) in the text of the novel. At times, I've been so excited by what I was writing about, the words are very difficult to decipher. Would anyone else find it of interest? I suppose not. The ramblings of an unpublished novelist. But the awful thing is—*I* find it interesting. Mind you, I find everything I've ever written interesting, even the one-act play about a giant crab terrorising a London suburb and its inhabitants. I get them out of the drawer sometimes and find them, in places, genuinely moving. Even funnier than the actual texts are the annotations in the margin—on the one-acter about the crab I've written "Poss. make Rat or Beetle?", although what a change of animal would have done for the plot I wouldn't like to say. A fond farewell to all my littleness—a farewell to *Dames In Gold Brocade*, a musical based on a Marxist interpretation of the life of Catherine de Medici: farewell to *Grub Street Here I Come*, a satirical novel about literary London, including a sinister and shadowy figure, called Luis d'Orsain, the spider at the centre of the literary web. So shadowy and sinister is d'Orsain that his hair changes colour four times in the course of the narrative, and he is, at various times, described as "squat", "huge" and "astonishingly lithe". Farewell to them all. I shall make a giant bonfire of the lot. *Dr Beamish's Desertion*, a novel about some Polish spies who infiltrate a London advertising agency in order to obtain hard currency for their masters in Warsaw; *The Forfeit*, a stream of consciousness narrative about a film director who has a heart attack while watching his award-winning commercial; and finally *The Garden*, a work loosely based on the work of Franz Kafka that I cannot understand *any* of. Considering I devoted a whole summer holiday to it, that seems to be a devastating indictment of my continuity as a person. Farewell though, farewell to the lot of them.

For I know I'll never be a writer. Not ever. There isn't going to be a seventeenth novel or play or poem or anything of the kind. That was at the root of the trouble between me and Ellen—even if reading the novel confirmed her suspicions, I think she always had an idea that I was wasting my time. And, as she said this afternoon, that meant she was losing respect for me. Our relationship is based, to a large extent, on leaving each other alone, on allowing the other partner to get on with what he or she wants to do. But I couldn't bear it if I felt she was spending all her afternoons crocheting or going to coffee mornings, and I suppose, to her, this study door was the way through to a prison. No one likes having a prison on the premises.... So no more books, Martin, no more books. O.K.?

We really are at the end of a phase aren't we? I suppose I now need some new way of keeping myself occupied. Well—for a start, I shall keep away from the literary pages of newspapers, full of photos of talentless twenty-five-year-olds with captions like "Rod Steerman: Brilliant Prose". I will take more interest in what goes on in the front end of weekly journals and the main body of daily newspapers—strikes, wars, demonstrations, etc. (Memo to self: What is the Women's Movement and Can Men Join It?) If I'm joining society I suppose I'd better find out about it. A lot of sex in straightforward positions. Possibly football, if I can get my chest reflated and find time to work out the rules. *Certainly* Car Maintenance and Beer Drinking With Men.

How to face people? Easy. On meeting young prick at party describing self as "novelist" say "Oh? Is that interesting?" On meeting older and more well established prick, say "I like your work very much indeed," whether or not I have read same. Give impression, as I say this, that I regard him in much the same light as the man who comes to do my central heating. Possibly even juicier ploy, when I have boned up on Marx and Engels and all this stuff Ellen keeps droning on about, will be to say "The novel is dead. I'm only *really* interested in the working class." If I say this often enough I may get to believe it and thus will be able to enjoy evening getting paralytic in the local pub with clear conscience. (Memo to self: Maybe I do believe it and that's why I can't be bothered to write the novel. Result? Ellen and I at Party meetings, arm in arm, planning the Revolution. "Comrades Ellen and Martin Steel are awarded the full text of Lenin's *Two Steps Forward One Step Back* in RUSSIAN as award for best attendance at Party meetings in Brixton area. Hooray.")

Only one problem remains. How to get back at enemies, people who have Put Me Down (especially girls and minor officials in the Nationalised Industries). In the absence of physical strength, I think the answer must be, hand in hand with the new Marxist Steel, a sudden flowering of the personality, a way with the vicious crack, so that I become the Most Feared Dinner Guest in London. Or the least invited I suppose —no matter. Hand-to-hand combat now where it's needed— no considered stuff. Same goes for Ellen. (Spiders under her bed? Hide in bathroom with light off after Dracula film on late-nite T.V? Browbeat her at dinner parties with wide range of newly acquired political info?) Oh, people at parties will point me out as a man who could have written a brilliant book, but decided that it wasn't worth the effort. Some will start a rumour that the manuscript is circulating, in typescript, around the Top Ten People in the country. I will not publicly deny this. Hickey will seek to phone me. I will be better looking too—time previously spent writing will now be passed in Guys 'n' Gals, a salon for hair in the Fulham Road. I will buy new jackets, new pairs of trousers. I may well get into astrology. I may even actively campaign *against* the Arts, proposing drastic cuts in subsidies to all nationalised theatres, the abolition of all fringe groups and the dismemberment of our major orchestras. "Sure—", I'll say, when asked about my mission in life, "I could write a book, anyone could write a book. But I'm afraid the day of the aesthete has passed. The best thing to do with our few remaining practitioners in the Arts is to round them up into a good-sized marquee and then set light to it. What we need now is more Real People, men and women who are prepared to face life, not run away from it." Another excellent technique here will be to admire fulsomely very bad (and popular) situation comedies on T.V. "Yeah," I shall say to up and coming dramatists, "but have you seen *The Grummits*? A brilliant comedy of manners *and* showing to thirteen million people. That's communication." The fact that both I and the up and coming dramatists know that *The Grummits* is a load of old rope makes no difference. The gesture is all. And now?

I will draw a line under this, the last page of my manuscript, tie up the pages neatly, and confide the thing to the bottom right-hand drawer, lock it, and then throw the key to the back of one of our cupboards. Maybe I'll find it again when I'm fifty and be amused to read about this rather absurd young man, so full of bitterness and irrelevant ambitions. I look round my study for what seems like the last time. There's something sad about it— the coffee cup at the edge of the desk, a cigarette stub in the saucer, the picture of Greece, hung to the left of the window, the twenty or thirty pencils and Biros, jammed into a tin on the windowledge. This room has been consecrated to something useless—from now on it'll be a sensible place. I'll come in here to pay Gas Bills, sort through Accounts, check out my Mortgage Number, write letters to my mother ... the last time, the last time! But how pleasant it is to confide this to the page, to watch the ink blacken the paper!

The gramophone has been switched off. I hear Ellen climbing the stairs. She pauses on the landing. Wondering whether to come in and say goodnight. Decides not to—she knows I'll be with her very soon. Oswald's door bangs, and the wind, still blowing round the house, hurls a dustbin against the wall further down the street. There are no lights in the opposite house, no voices, no radios, no parties, no cars starting, no sirens in the distance—nothing except the wind in the empty street, the moon on the rainy pavement. Quiet as the grave. When I go in to Ellen she will still be awake. We'll lie in the dark, chatting about nothing, the way we used to do before I got caught up in that book. *That* book—I can say it like that—so casually and so dismissively. We'll celebrate this, my farewell to an art that never got off the ground. It's over. No more writing, no more writing I swear.

Well, what are you waiting for Steel? Put the pen down. Go on, put the pen down.